Marriage Made in Heaven

When we say I will

Kevin & Amanda Wood

ISBN 978-1-9993230-0-4 (Paperback)

First edition 2019
10 9 8 7 6 5 4 3 2 1 0

Contents

Foreword

What is a 'vow'? A vow is shared in almost every circumstance and conversation because it is a promise, an oath, a covenant, a commitment, affirmation, assurance or more. Most of us equate a vow to the bride and groom exchange during the wedding ceremony. However, we use vows, or promises, when purchasing a home, buying an automobile or simply giving a commitment for an appointment. Vow is used 77 times in the New International Version (NIV) of the Bible; mostly in the Old Testament book of Numbers. Interestingly, more than half of those verses speak about husbands and wives and vows.

Ok, so let's talk about the wedding vows and their importance. When my wife, Mae and I are mentoring an engaged couple, we ask them what expectations they have of marriage. Most respond with a surprised, clueless, look upon their faces because they've usually not had that conversation, or thought for that matter. After that discussion we lead into the meaning (or their interpretation) of the vows to one another. We have found, like Kevin & Amanda, that most couples have only the knowledge of the 'traditional' reciting and not the in-depth meaning of what they are actually promising to each other. As we explore, and unpack each element of the vows, most couples will share they have no idea of the special commitment they are making legally, spiritually or emotionally to their future spouse. Some couples elect to create their personalized vows based on ancestry, culture and even how they intend to walk through life together. This book has elevated the meaning of those vows to a wonderful level that helps to express a couples' intent to flourish and achieve success to the full potential they expect of marriage.

Kevin and Amanda have taken the definition of vows to a greater level of clarification. Speaking and referring to marriage as 'Us" and "We" verses "I' or "Me" is a powerful testimony to the unity of the flesh in Genesis 2:24, "That is why a man leaves his father and mother and is united to his wife, and they become one flesh." They lead by example, using Biblical principles and scripture to demonstrate God's meaning of the wedding vows. We share their recognition of the importance of commitment to Christ and the 'vow' to Him in a couples' declaration on the wedding day.

Chuck Dettman www.todayspromise.org.

Chuck, along with his wife Mae, are authors of 'The Marriage Journey', A Flight Plan to Your Healthy Marriage.' They have mentored for more than 27 years and just celebrated 50 years of Marriage

Acknowledgments

Writing this first book together has been both challenging and an adventure. Firstly, we would like to thank our family for their encouragement, particularly our sons, Adam & Gareth, who had to put up with busyness in our ministry to couples. Thanks to Rev Huw Davies, Nicky & Sila Lee (the marriagecourses.org) and Richard & Katherine Hill (careforthefamily.org.uk) for inspiring us to get into working with married couples.

We would like to thank all our friends at restorationblueprint.com for their considerable encouragement during the writing—we love you all. In particular we would like to thank Anne Vyce and Sue Hughes for their help in proof reading.

We are very grateful for the advice and support of Chuck & Mae Dettman (Florida, USA) of todayspromise.org and Roy & Lainey Hitchman (Hungary) of hitchedtogether.com in the aspects of book publishing. Thanks also to Rainer Knack at RelateWorks.com (Germany) for his guidance in making ministry plans.

We would also like to thank our friends David & Lorrie McIntyre (Georgia, USA) of OneHeartBeatGA.com for their unending encouragement and our new friends at (timeformarriage.org.uk) for their shared passion in helping married couples.

Special mention goes to Rev Richard & Helen Salmon with Graham & Carolyn Campbell for believing in us and being a support, when providing courses for married and engaged couples in the early days.

We would also like to honour John & Stella Wood (Kevin's parents) who have been married for more than 65 years. Throughout that time they have consistently modelled devotion and commitment as an example to all.

There are too many others to name who have blessed us on our journey but we thank you and our Lord and Saviour, Jesus Christ for all that you have done and continue to do.

Preface

We first started putting ideas down for this book, back in 2012, on a rainy day whilst staying on holiday in a cosy cottage in Cornwall, in the South West of England. It wasn't a whim but rather an opportunity to finally put pen to paper about an aspect we had often found neglected by the writers of books on marriage.

Why a book on marriage vows? The marriage vows are really the starting point from where marriage comes into being. Up until this point the couple's relationship has been developing and hopefully growing, but finally on the wedding day those marriage vows are formally, legally and most importantly, publicly made.

These vows are declared solemnly—although outwardly they are made joyfully. The vows are not to be entered into lightly as they are like no other promises that we are likely to make during our lives.

In this book we will attempt to explain our understanding of how these vows—and our ability to keep them, affect our endurance and our hope to be forever loved and loving. All too often, individuals will forget the depth of those promises and put the success of the marriage down to chance. A common misconception is that one is lucky if one finds the 'perfect soul-mate'. We are of the firm belief that whilst there is an element of wisdom in choosing our life partner, it is not about our spouse; rather it is that our commitment to these vows is top priority. This is what builds the marriage relationship. We want you to know God in your marriage. We hope to inspire you to seek Him out if you do not know Him yet.

We have based this book on the 'traditional' vows from the Church of England marriage service (see Appendix A.1) We believe they have stood the test of time and closely relate to God's view and intention of the marriage covenant. You may notice that we have written the words "I Will" on the front cover and not "I Do", as so many people believe. When we say "I Will" it is a statement of intent—a promise of commitment—a covenant promise. (Ezekiel Chapters 36-39) We are fully aware that many couples do not actually use these particular vows in their wedding service. However, we want to emphasise the importance of making a promise and publicly stating one's intentions of love and loyalty to one another. This is powerful and hugely important and is witnessed by God who is actually everywhere! Whether in a church or any other building or surrounding—wherever your wedding has, or is, to take place. (See Proverbs 15:3)

Life is a journey. As you join us on this journey through these chapters, whether you are contemplating marriage, engaged, selecting vows or have been married for a short or long time, we hope you will be able to identify the truths that will enlighten you with a broader view of why the marriage vows should play such a big part in the determination of marital harmony and success.

Introduction

This book has been written to encourage and guide couples on the Marriage vows most popularly used in Western Christian contemporary culture. For that reason, we have deliberately not chosen to delve too deeply into the origins of the institution of Marriage or the history of the most commonly known vows as expressed in the Church of England marriage service. We may tackle these historical origins in another book. However, the Christian Church Marriage service is largely based on Thomas Cranmer's Book of Common Prayer, written almost 500 years ago in 1549. It is widely understood that Thomas Cranmer based these words on the Sarum Marriage Liturgy and York Rituals that date back further. Although the Common Book of Prayer has seen a few revisions along the way, the basic vows as highlighted in the Chapter Titles 2 to 7 of this book have largely been unchanged since medieval times. We believe God has allowed these vows to be created and be used for the purposes of His Kingdom. These core vows have been, and continue to be, used by Protestant and Catholic denominations and are recognised by the State in many English-speaking nations. The purpose of this book is not to get into religious theological debate about whether marriage is a sacrament or not. As we see it, marriage can lead to a deeper experience of the presence of God and is approved by Him. Millions of couples have entered into this Covenant relationship over hundreds of years and it has blessed society and family life, irrespective of whether those married fully appreciated the spiritual significance. It is with all this in mind that we hope the readers see benefits, or be reminded of the alignment of those vows with Biblical scripture. Acknowledging God first as our guide, in how we love and why we have committed our lives to each other until death, helps us to make sense of our relationship in marriage. We say, "your will be done on Earth as it is in Heaven."

You will notice two font styles for the main text. One is for Kevin the other is for Amanda (Mandy).

Chapter 1

The Proposal

'Lord, direct me throughout my journey so I can experience your plans for my life. Reveal the life-paths that are pleasing to you.' (Psalm 25:4 TPT)

The journey to engagement started with Mandy and I dating—or 'going out' with each other as we called it. From my perspective, I suppose, the entrance to marriage came from a decision to 'pop the question' by asking, "will you marry me?" Although the woman sometimes does the asking these days, this is still a fairly rare occurrence and not something we would advocate as being preferable. Mandy will be explaining why it is important for the man to make the decision in the next chapter.

I remember realising that marriage was not to be entered into lightly and was one of life's biggest decisions. It was up there with what career to follow and where to live. But

I would say that the most important decision is to whom you are going to marry.

Mandy and I had talked about our suitability as life partners on numerous occasions and I had even hinted on the subject within our first month of dating, whilst on an evening stroll along the river Teign in Devon. We never really mentioned the 'M' word, for fear of spoiling the proposal as a romantic event in itself—or indeed, 'putting the cart before the horse.' In other words, asking before we were ready to commit. (See Song of Songs 3:5)

How did I decide then? Did I wake up one morning compelled to ask? No! It was more of a gradual decision based on my increased awareness and knowledge of how Mandy behaved, our shared interests, values and sense of humour.

I selected a suitable date to ask Mandy to marry me. We had pre-arranged to go out for a meal at a 'posh' restaurant in Salisbury, Wiltshire (U.K) to celebrate the fact that we had been going out with each other for exactly one year. I wanted that date to be memorable and romantic. We had already chosen the venue together and unknown to me, Mandy had also prepared a surprise for me that evening. I think it was safe to say that Mandy was totally unaware that my surprise would be 'popping the question!'

Having set the date of the proposal in my mind, did I have any doubts? Absolutely not! Did I have reservations? Well, yes. Not about Mandy, but more about whether the venue would be suitable or that my delivery of 'the question,' would be romantic enough!

I believed that it would be the right thing to do, to tell my parents and gather confirmation that they approved of Mandy. They handled my enquiry of them superbly. They affirmed my choice but gave me no feelings of obligation to follow through and were eager for me to listen to my heart by not placing any importance or burden for me to take their advice. It was clearly my decision, and I am grateful for their counsel. I know they loved me enough to know that whatever I did would receive their blessing.

A few weeks before the proposal date, I went on a pilgrimage to a clearing amidst a small copse of trees on a hill overlooking the Exe valley. I had been to this beautiful spot on my own twice before. Once when I was struggling to decide on my choice for study at school and again when choosing a University. This was the big one. I needed to feel happy in myself that I had made the right choice. I didn't have a faith in God at that time of my life but I recognised His existence and felt I needed to speak with Him about my situation. No booming voice but rather a small, still voice in my spirit—a peace found amongst the isolation of this spot. I felt a gentle breeze blowing across my face as I looked across the vista.

I now know that there was no similar opportunity for such meditation and revelation for Mandy. Difficult for any woman to make an on the spot decision about such a life changing course, made all the worse these days by many men thinking that they have to make ever increasingly sophisticated, exotic, extravagant and often very public proposals. (I am sure you have all seen the YouTube videos.)

What did my proposal look like? Did I go down on one knee or have an engagement ring in my back pocket? Nope! I ventured to ask the big question across the dinner table at the rather small and intimate restaurant. The trouble was that this particular venue was unexpectedly quiet and our allotted table was slap-bang in the middle of the room. Everyone around us was speaking in whispers and each time I was about to start the prelude speech, to my proposal, the waitress would come over and interrupt. Tension was mounting. Time was running out. Would I miss the perfect moment? I took charge of the situation. I announced that I had something important to say. I felt slightly moved emotionally because a few days before I had briefly considered the possibility that she would say "No." I would say that I was ninety-five percent sure that she would say "Yes," but through my rose-tinted spectacles, I hadn't really worked out an exit strategy. The potential ramifications could have been huge. Failure, rejection and ultimately a vote of no confidence in us could have resulted in a wounding, if not a cessation, of our relationship.

I finally came to the bit in my speech when I asked, "Will you marry me?" There followed the longest few seconds of silence in my life. Had she heard the soft tones in my voice? Was there a problem? On reflection, in my eagerness to extract an answer, I had completely overlooked the fact that Mandy needed time to overcome the emotion of the moment. Time to collect her thoughts. In my heart, I interpreted a hesitation as doubt or uncertainty as to whether I would make a suitable husband. I had failed to realise that a proposal, for women, is a bigger deal than it is for men. I had had plenty of hours to consider things but was expecting an instantaneous response from Mandy.

I can't imagine how difficult it must be for a woman to wait for a proposal of marriage. If a woman says "No" to the first man who asks, she may wonder if she will ever receive another proposal. Some women are in love with the romance of the wedding day more than accepting the possibility of remaining happily unmarried. For others it could be a project to turn their boyfriend into the person they would really like to marry.

This silence probably only lasted three or four seconds. I could see Mandy's eyes looking lovingly across the table at me but no audible sound was coming from her lips. All was not lost! I couldn't bear the silence a moment longer and blurted out a rhetorical question in the form of one word "Well?"

Mandy's eyes said it all. Her words came out a little choked. Was this it? Was this really happening? It was and so her answer was a heartfelt "YES!"

I believe that, like most other little girls, I share the memory of playing weddings and dressing up as a bride throughout my early childhood. I can actually recall a particular occasion, at the tender age of six or seven, being 'married off' to the little boy next door until it was my friend's 'turn' to be married to him, only minutes later! Many a net curtain was acquired for the purpose of covering ourselves with a veil and of course we needed my mum's high-heeled shoes to complete the look. Sometimes I would spend hours in my bedroom happily playing with my dolls and marrying them off to each other. When Kevin made his proposal, my first immediate thought was "this is it, this is the moment I have been waiting for but is this the man I really want to spend the rest of my life with?"

It was exactly a year before that Kevin proposed a different question. I was dancing with my best friend at the local Discothèque, when I heard a voice and saw this guy approach us. "Excuse me but would you like to dance with me?" My first thought then was, 'why have I got the short guy?' His friend had asked my friend and he appeared to be of similar height to me. It was dark and I was wearing very high heels! Poor Kevin! He is not that short really (Aren't we fickle sometimes?) When I actually took the time to look at him, I could see that he was a very attractive bloke and that I had got the better of the two men after all. It didn't take long before we were experiencing our first kiss at the end of the evening and throughout that first year, we grew more and more in love.

We had to part only six months into our relationship due to our different career paths. Kevin went off to University in Surrey and I started my nurse training in Salisbury, Wiltshire. This 'separation' was in some way a good testing ground for both of us, challenging our values and deep held beliefs about what we considered important at that time. I quickly found Kevin to be an extremely passionate, caring and sensitive person.

When I was contemplating giving up my nurse training, as I really wasn't enjoying it, and trying to get a sense of how I felt about things, I considered the choice of being with Kevin or staying put. I remember accusing him of putting pressure on me in my decision making and controlling my thoughts. To him it was a 'no brainer'- I either wanted to be with him or I didn't. But I wanted him to acknowledge my feelings too. We had our first major argument. Letters and recorded cassette tapes passed between us. Please note this was way before voicemail, Skype and text messaging was available! You had to make more of an effort to make your feelings known years ago. Putting a coat on, when it was cold, to go out to a telephone box for example, only to find it occupied or not working, tested our relationship. Deep down I knew I loved him too much and I enjoyed his attentions towards me. He gave me that sense of security and made me feel special and needed—an emotion I now know all women crave in a marital relationship—so it was natural for me to tap into this and find Kevin was the one for me. By the way, I decided to give up my nursing and start a new job, which I got soon afterwards.

As the question, "will you marry me?" left Kevin's lips, I found myself in this excited 'bubble,' in the realisation of the situation. A mix of feelings pervaded my thoughts with "so this is it, is he really the guy of my dreams?" to "yes, because he loves me and has shown me by his actions as well as his words." I murmured a "yes" but my excitement caused me to choke so that my mouth opened to speak but nothing came out! Kevin was led to say "well?" which sort of jolted me into breathing again, as if he had resuscitated me and I was actually able to verbalise my joy and acceptance.

I was just about to tuck into my Black Forest gateau when he started his speech. Now it had lost its appeal and became this insignificant pudding. My eyes were now feasting on my handsome fiancé—my husband to be.

Let's Pray

1. Lord, let us not lean on our own understanding but in all things acknowledge You—pray for His good counsel by seeking the counsel of Godly people who are already married.
2. Seek His peace in your heart—do not do what the world says is the right thing to do. If the Holy Spirit does not leave His peace, love and joy about this person you are considering for marriage, then don't marry them! Remember 'marriage is not to be entered into lightly.'
3. Give thanks for the opportunity God gave you to propose/accept your partner. Thank Him for that memorable moment when you chose each other.

Chapter 2

To Have and to Hold

"Haven't you read," he replied, "that at the beginning the Creator 'made them male and female', and said, 'For this reason a man will leave his father and mother and be united to his wife, and the two will become one flesh?' (Matthew 19:4-6 NIV)

The sun was shining quite brightly through the canopy of leaves. It was like the diamonds in an engagement ring—twinkling, flickering and hi-lighting the bridal path that was lined with various trinkets and flowers. It was a garden wedding like the first wedding that ever took place. At the end of the grassy aisle was a tent—with a few more stationary onlookers. The tent was a triangle shape, enough to give shelter and act as a covering.

I was six or seven at the time and my friend Abby, also seven years old, was smiling at me as she came up this leafy trail with her right arm tucked into the reluctant, hanging limb of Stephen's left elbow—he was the little six-year old boy next door.

"We are gathered here today to, to, to...," I stuttered and looked up from my little scribbled note to see them giggling and looking rather sheepishly at each other. "You mustn't laugh! This is very serious!" I rebuked. "Now say after me will you take...?" Stephen interrupted, "Do I have to?"

Okay, so this was children 'play acting'. The stage was set for a beautiful wedding—a garden wedding but here the chairs were laid out with toys and teddies for guests. Pretty things and flowers adorned the area where the ceremony would take place and the bride wore a long flowing veil—her mother's net curtain. I was way ahead of my time believing I could be a female Vicar! Abby and I were very aware of our destiny, as little women, that one day we hoped we were going to get married. Stephen, on the other hand, didn't hang around and made a quick exit back to his house for more manly pursuits of playing soldiers, cowboys or football perhaps?

That tent—the one that was at the end of the bridal path—can you see it? It was the shape of a triangle. A great analogy of how blessed a couple can be if they have God in their marriage. What do I mean by this? Well, a traditional tent looks like a triangle with its three sides. In ancient times, nomads including the great patriarchs like Abraham, lived in tents made of goat and camel hair, which enabled the fabric to give shade, to breathe in warm weather and contract in the winter rains. So, marriage as a tent is not only a visible symbol, illustrating the strength of God, with the triple braided guy ropes that are dug deep and are strong to hold, but also being secure in His love by the canopy of His protection through three ways—God, the Father, His Son Jesus and the Holy Spirit. A three-sided triangle can also represent God at the top with Husband on the right and Wife on the left. Only He can join us as two imperfect people and redeem us, in our marriage, by Christ's death on the cross. He helps us in our weak areas so we learn how to love and be loved. (Ephesians 1:7). In the Old Testament, the 'tent' of God was called a Tabernacle or Sanctuary where the presence of God would dwell. Indeed David, in the Psalms, asks the question, "Lord, who dares to dwell with you?" (Psalm 15:1 TPT). And again in Psalm 61:4 (NLT) "Let me live forever in your sanctuary, safe beneath the shelter of your wings." In a tent, especially God's tent, there is that sense of intimacy which we affirm when we declare 'to have and to hold from this day forward', a picture of infinite intimacy in God's presence. The book of Ecclesiastes chapter 4 verses 9,10 (NLT) says 'Two people can accomplish more than twice as much as one...' 'If one person falls, the other can reach out and help...'These verses suggest that two people, in this case in marriage, are better able to serve each other and work together more effectively than alone. They are supportive and dependable, feel secure and provide staying power with the other's encouragement. However, better still is three 'for a triple braided cord is not easily broken' (Eccl. 4:12 NLT). Our tent has to be securely held down, otherwise it is at risk from being blown away by 'ill winds'—guy-ropes are designed to add stability and are at least triple braided to give strength.

Now, if two is the minimum number required for a relationship and where 'many' people come together is called a group, a team can consist of two or more and it's the 'team work' that I am going to illustrate here and explain why it is so important in a relationship.

> *'Then make me truly happy by agreeing wholeheartedly with each other, loving one another, and working together with one heart and purpose...For God is working in you, giving*

you the desire to obey him and the power to do what pleases him.' (Philippians 2:2,13 NLT)

It took 'team work'—working together in one common purpose—to get our tents up securely before darkness fell.

Kevin and I would sometimes say to each other, as well as to our friends and family "Well we just don't do camping—we are not tent people!" There was a line in a film about a dog, called 'Beethoven,' where I believe the dad said something like "We are not dog people—we don't do dogs!", so we kind of said in the same vein, "We don't do tents—we are not tent people!"

However, when our two boys got to that age of needing adventure and the opportunity to step out on their own and away from the full clutches of mum and dad—without actually being completely alone—you know, making them feel they are independent when they aren't exactly? Well, having their own two-man tent separate from our mother tent seemed to be a good idea.

There had to be some rules, the main one being that a camping holiday would only take place on a sunny weekend at a campsite of our choosing. On this particular occasion we had to pitch up on a slight slope, which meant our feet faced downhill and we slept, head end, nearer the fence that surrounded the site.

I woke up one sunny Sunday morning to this munching sound and heavy breathing right by my ear! Kevin was sleeping peacefully—so it wasn't him!

"What on earth is that noise?" I thought. I was wide awake by now. It then became obviously clear that a horse had decided to complete his breakfast by enjoying the luscious grass on the other side of the fence from our tent. The noise of his munching was quite intrusive and at first, before I had identified the source, a little frightening actually and it seemed like he might invade our space. I was so glad that our tent 'protected' us from this beautiful animal, who seemed totally oblivious to us and wasn't as close as it sounded!

A tent is, as we have said before, a symbol of God's protection. You can also cleave together in all weathers like we did on a windy beach once—but that's another story! It brings intimacy with strong ties as you hold fast and there must be synergy.

Synergy is when you have two or more things working together in a particularly fruitful way creating an effect that is better than working separately—having God's spirit in the relationship enables a married couple to work more effectively as a team towards the same goal with common purpose. '...Since they are no longer two but one...for God has joined them together.' (Matthew 19:6 NLT). They are working together at their relationship, sharing, submitting to one another and trying to see things from the same perspective. With God in the relationship, this is possible because He joined them together. We have noted that God's tent is seen as a protective covering in marriage and, interestingly, the Bible simply mentions that it is the place where the marriage of Isaac and Rebekah took place. 'And Isaac brought Rebekah into his mother's tent and she became his wife' (Gen 24:67 NLT).

The fussiness of a wedding with all the frilliness, fads and fancies doesn't make a marriage. Where the marriage ceremony takes place, yes even in a tent, doesn't make a marriage. "What do you mean?" I hear you ask. Well, only God can make a marriage by His joining of the couple so that 'no man may separate'[i]. When you say in public and before God—and He is present wherever the wedding takes place—"Everything I have and everything I am, I give to you," and "to be by your side, to hold fast to you," is more than just a promise to your spouse. It's certainly more than a contract, it's a vow to God, a covenant promise, that you should become one in mind, spirit and body. You are no longer 'I' but a 'we' and 'us'. You no longer go it alone but together with God, who not only joins us together but is a witness to our promise. (Malachi 2:14,15).

When the Bible uses the phrase 'to cleave' in some older translations, it literally means in Hebrew, to be 'glued' together! (Gen 2:24)

In his book, 'Married for God',[ii] the author Christopher Ash refers to Jesus from the gospels of Mark (10:7-9) and Matthew (19:4-6) by explaining that 'Marriage involves leaving parents, so that husband and wife become 'next of kin' to one another. It involves a 'cleaving' or 'holding fast', a word which combines passion with permanence. And it results in a 'one flesh' union, which is a joining done by God.'— that is a permanent fixture! We really have to be ready to take that step. It is not about the wedding. When we declare that we are to 'have and to hold' each other, a picture of intimacy infinitum, we are that permanent team helping each other. It's a wonderful feeling when you take the time to see yourselves as a team, working together and enjoying each other in the tent of your marriage with God. This establishes the foundation of marriage—but let's go back to that garden.

Life appears simple and straightforward when we are children. We tend to dwell on the wedding day and all that entails but as we get older we have other things to consider. I believe that most people like the idea of marriage. It's taking the plunge! It's going down on one knee and saying "Yes". It's 'jumping the broomstick'—an old African custom symbolising a new life together as a married couple, that still survives amongst African Americans today and in other parts of the world.

But have we really considered the commitment part? Maybe we have. Are we hesitating? Or if we are already married, we may be thinking about that vow, "to have and to hold". What does it mean to you now?

Decisions—we make many small ones and large ones; and fairly insignificant ones—but also very important ones— like the proposal of marriage. You are at that point in your relationship where you are considering proposing to your girlfriend or indeed you are the girl who has been asked that special question, 'will you marry me?' It is a very significant moment, an important decision. The marriage service declares that marriage should not be entered into lightly. Why is that do you think? Why is the proposal given so much credence, so much acclaim? The guys (usually) who do the proposing, set up the stage, choose the place and prepare their speech. Everything has to be 'right' in the hope that their partner will make the 'right' decision to say "yes."

That decision, though, has to be right for both parties. It really mustn't be entered into lightly because deep down we all want that decision to hold fast for the rest of our lives. Like it says 'from this day forward,' not just for the wedding day. The Bible says in Joshua 24:15 (NLT)....'then choose today whom you will serve....' And in verse 22, 'You are accountable for this decision.'

Sadly, over the years, more and more couples are not making this decision to get married but stay in a cohabitating relationship. No decision is made about this relationship, how long they intend to be together, what each party is going to bring into the relationship—or not, when things don't go to plan. So, nothing gets decided and they find themselves with life's consequences making the decision for them. For a man to make the decision, taking the lead and expressing his love for his future wife, is a very powerful thing. If a man makes the decision to marry, makes the proposal after thinking it through, then he has decided in his heart not just his head. He sees his wife-to-be as a potential mate and mother of his children perhaps. He sees how she compliments him, supports him, challenges him and shares his humour but, most importantly, how she honours and respects him—then he knows he has made the right decision. When this happens, the marriage is more likely to work.

To 'have and to hold' has that ring of permanence that encircles the two people who have taken that decision. Both have given themselves to each other and the rings are a symbol of that exchange. It is not only a decision made between the couple by themselves, but a public commitment before God, telling the world that you are setting up a permanent relationship with one another. "I have you and you have me—we are holding on together!"

When Kevin and I came out of the church, we were surrounded, as you are, by all our friends and family. The photographer was trying to arrange us for the necessary photographic poses that he wanted to make. One of them was a very memorable one of us in the waiting car that was going to take us on to the reception. I say memorable because years later we tried to set up the same pose again for an anniversary picture. A sort of 'then and now' picture show! On our wedding day, Kevin got in the car first and then I carefully followed and sat down beside him, having swivelled around and readjusted all the frills and voluminous bundle of lace and taffeta, making sure I hadn't sat on my pink roses that my mum had sewn on to the bottom frill. She had made the whole outfit.

The photographer, at that moment, asked me to get as close as I could and cuddle up to "your husband!" It was the first time I had heard that word applied towards me. It was meant for me. I was a wife! It was a magical moment of feeling really proud. Having and holding that 'title' meant that my fiancé was now legally my husband and not just my partner and soul-mate.

'Marriage should be honoured by all' (Hebrews 13:4 NIV). It is a status that we should embrace and something that we touch on again in a later chapter. It is how we show our understanding of our marital status that gives the words 'to have and to hold from this day forward,' more meaning, more gravitas. How do you honour your marriage relationship? How do you value marriage as a whole? Well, before you can consider those questions, maybe there are some other 'pointers' to ponder on before making the decision to marry at all. I refer to Walter Trobisch, author of 'I Married You.'[iii] He considers six tests of love that he believes couples should ask themselves to see if they are the marrying kind.

The Sharing test - understanding that you are marrying the other person with their concerns and feelings being placed before your own. I remember our eldest son saying once that he couldn't marry yet because he was still too selfish. I thought that was very sensible.

The Respect test - are you proud of each other and truly value each other? We will look at this more closely in a later chapter.

The Strength test - are you filled with the energy, excitement and creativity when you are with this person that you love? Do you want to accomplish more with this person? Or do you feel zapped of energy, there is no strength left to pursue the relationship?

The Habit test - accepting each other's differences, even the annoying ones! Love accepts another's habits with the understanding that you can't change them. Do you actually like each other?

The Quarrel test - can you survive conflict and resolve it effectively, coming out knowing that you are still on the same team? That you still like each other and are able to understand each other's points of view? Can you forgive each other?

Some people say that they have never quarrelled. They are either lying or they are not really living as a couple but as flatmates—or worst still, it is all bubbling under the surface and will eventually erupt over something simple. Similar to the story we heard about a couple who claimed to never argue, then one

Christmas an issue came up involving the wrapping paper. Then 'whoosh' a tirade of deep hurts came flooding out that had been stored up. The author, Walter Trobisch says that he believes it is quarrels that need to be experienced instead of sex before marriage!

Finally, the Time test - how long have you been going out with each other? The dating game is an opportunity to get to know each other without the constraints of sexual intimacy, which puts pressure on a relationship before it has God's blessing in marriage. Kevin and I had known each other for one year and dated sometimes at a distance when we left home to follow our respective career paths. This did put pressure on us to have a more intimate relationship but we held fast until we became engaged. We decided to live together then, as I had moved to work near Kevin and it made sense to share the rent. We didn't appreciate the spiritual significance of our decision to start a more intimate relationship as we hadn't become Christians and couldn't know what the Bible said. We didn't fully appreciate that God created marriage. That it was His plan from the beginning. But the past cannot be changed and we know we would do things differently now. As a couple, however, we have been able to ask for His forgiveness and He has blessed our marriage over the years.

If that is your story or similar, then we hope you too have made your peace with each other, yourself and with God—forgiving yours and each other's past sexual experiences.

Sexual encounters with others, prior to meeting with our husband or wife, will create what is referred to as, a 'soul-tie' connection with them. This will be with us long after the former relationship has ended—however fleeting it may have been. This is because sexual intimacy is a bonder that transcends the sexual act and stays with us emotionally in our soul. Recognising that spiritual aspect of a sexual relationship is important because we can then take our past to God, who then redeems us, so we can now look forward and not backward towards a continual, fulfilling, married life.

What you now have (and bring into this marriage), you can now hold (on to each other), from this day forward.

Let's Pray

1. For God's protective 'tent' over our marriage—to be a part of our triangle.
   Thank Him for His redemptive power, through Christ's death and resurrection. That we may hand over any of our problems and differences to Him because He knows us

better than we know ourselves. Let us pray for a new start every day.

2. Ask God to forgive us if we have just married because it was just a nice idea and a wedding was a fun thing to do.
3. Ask Him for His plan for your marriage.
4. For the courage to get married if we are still living together.
5. Let us pray for God's forgiveness if you have given yourself to somebody else or even to each other, sexually, before marriage. Only He can redeem your past.

Chapter 3

For Better for Worse

'Clothe yourselves with tender-hearted mercy, kindness, humility, gentleness, and patience. You must make allowances for each other's faults and forgive the person who offends you.' (Colossians 3:12-13 NLT)

We have a little 'communication' card that we must have bought or had given to us years ago. It is pinned on to our notice board, on the wall of our kitchen, and repositioned regularly by the many holes in it where it has been re-pinned. It is called 'A Good Marriage.' I do not need to write out every verse but only those that I feel are relevant to this vow of acceptance, "For better, for worse".

'A good marriage must be created; It is never being too old to hold hands; It is having the capacity to forgive and forget; It is giving each other an atmosphere in which each can grow.

'For better or for worse'—what do you think about when you say that vow? Now be honest, most of us think immediately that it is about the other person being the worst. We are okay, of course, but we might have to put up with the possibility of '*them*' letting us down, putting up with the worst aspects of *their* personality or worse still! That's what I used to think— but let us turn it around. In the Bible it speaks of looking at life from a Godly perspective and changing the way you think.

> *'Do not conform any longer to the pattern of this world, but be transformed by the renewing of your mind.' (Romans 12:2 NIV)*

It is what is written at the end of the communication card that really spoke to me. "It's not about marrying the right person, it is being the right partner." Shouldn't it be me that brings the better part of myself and not the worst into the relationship? There was also the line "It is giving each other an atmosphere in which each can grow."

In the Bible St Paul encourages us to fill our minds with Heavenly thoughts and we are …'to get rid of anger, rage, malicious behaviour, slander and dirty language' (Colossians 3:8 NLT). Our attitude greatly affects our behaviour and as a consequence, the way we communicate. This has been found through extensive research by the American research group of Doctor John Gottman, to be a major cause of marital breakdown and supported by British Research director, Harry Benson of The Marriage Foundation and author of 'Let's Stick Together.'[iv]

St. Paul uses clothes, 'garments' as an allegory of attitude. Something we either put on or take off. The Message Bible speaks of 'that old life' being like …'a filthy set of ill-fitting clothes…' (Colossians 3:9 THE MESSAGE) Should we not then bring an atmosphere of kindness, encouragement and forgiveness into our marriages, and an attitude towards our husband or wife that shows we love them?

'Now you are dressed in a new wardrobe. Every item of your new way of life is custom-made by the creator, with his label on it, ...dress in the wardrobe that God picked out for you…' (Colossians 3:9,10,12).

We are called, or should I say divinely commanded, through Paul's words, in this letter to the Colossians, 'Wives understand and support your husbands'…. 'Husbands go all out in love for your wives' (THE MESSAGE Ch 3:18). In other translations, the word 'submit' is used for the wives and that the husbands must 'love your wives and never treat them harshly.' (NLT)

I think these other translations put it quite bluntly but it amounts to the same thing. It's all about our attitude towards one another. We are to completely devote ourselves to building each other up emotionally, in what we say, and helping each other, in what we do, so each partner enjoys the better times and shares the worst of times together.

It is an unfortunate consequence that, in parts of Western culture, there is such an emphasis placed on the importance of having to be 'happy all the time' and finding someone or something to blame if you are not! If you are not 'happy' then there must be something terribly wrong, whether that is to do with our homes, jobs, cars and our relationships, including our marriages. Couples have been known to say, "I just don't love him or her anymore—he or she doesn't make me happy." Now there is absolutely nothing wrong with wanting to be happy and have a cheerful disposition but we shouldn't expect our partners to make us happy and vice versa. No one should ever be placed under that level of expectation. Only God can meet our deepest needs. But it is good for us to be aware of our spouse's emotional and physical needs.

We were looking at attitudes earlier; how and what we bring into the marriage relationship and how we can help each other through the worst of times. We mustn't give up on our marriage if our husband or wife is not 'pulling their weight' in the relationship but there is a thin line between tolerating and accepting such behaviour. I believe the difference between tolerating and accepting, in marriage in particular, has something to do with emotional intimacy—that oneness that must be there for a couple's relationship to thrive and grow.

If we go back to the very beginning, back to the garden of Eden, God's work was not complete until He had made a suitable helper for Adam—a woman. He could have created her like He created Adam—from the dust of the earth. However, He chose to form her from the man's body. "At last!" Adam exclaims. (Genesis 2:23 NLT) "She is part of my own flesh and bone! Her name is woman because she was taken out of man." 'This explains why a man leaves his father and mother and is joined to his wife and the two are united into one' (Genesis 2:24 NLT). Marriage is God's illustration of symbolic oneness in relationship. A covenant relationship created by God that only He joins together. The question is: are we willing or committed to becoming one, not only in body but in mind and spirit also? What has this got to do with the vow 'for better, for worse'?

Let us look at the next verse in Genesis chapter 2. In verse 25, after God has joined them together, it says that although Adam and Eve were naked, neither of them felt any shame. Sin had not yet entered and therefore superiority, self-awareness and embarrassment were not present between them.

Many couples come into marriage as two single people. "Yeah! Right!" I hear you cry. I may have stated the obvious there but bear with me and let me repeat that. We come into marriage as two single people. Is that right or wrong? Well wrong, if we remain single minded. We should come together as a couple. We are not two halves and certainly not good or better halves! We are not fifty-fifty but one hundred per cent joined into a 'one-flesh' union. This 'one-flesh' union is not just about sex, I might add! That is just one other dimension—a very important one, of course, and does have a great effect on this concept of oneness. We must think of ourselves as one not two separate people in mind, body and spirit. That is also why, as an aside, there is an importance placed in being 'equally yoked.'

Intimacy—the word itself means to be open, deeply familiar and personal. That's very close and trusting. How can we be any of those things with our husband or wife without making ourselves vulnerable? That is why it is used to describe sexual relationships. In Latin, intimate or *intimus* means innermost. We share our innermost thoughts with the people we love and trust and to whom we can make ourselves vulnerable—our husband or wife. To be vulnerable, we have to 'know' each other enough to feel able to 'be naked and without shame' (v 25 NLT). Earlier Bible translations describe couples as 'knowing' each other. This is translated from the Ancient Hebrew text *'yada'* which describes an intimate knowledge of one another. It is the same word that is used when speaking of God's knowledge of us because he created us and wants us, too, to have an intimate knowledge of Him. (John 17:3) I believe that is why St. Paul describes marriage, like our relationship with Christ—deep, mysterious but wonderful.

When we come together in our knowledge of each other, both intimately and generally, there is that oneness between us that should allow a certain acceptance of each other's weak areas where we bring perceived 'worse' traits into the relationship. I mentioned earlier that I believe there is a difference between tolerating and accepting. I was reading a blog post the other day and a woman described her situation living with an alcoholic husband. She wrote about how she 'tolerates' his behaviour and that she 'puts up with him' and then admitted that she was miserable. Well, to me she is not bringing her best into the marriage by tolerating his abusive behaviour. He is abusing himself through drink and possibly abusing her as well; if not physically but certainly mentally.

To 'tolerate' in the dictionary means, 'enduring or permitting without any interference; enduring with suffering'. It seems to me that tolerating is just putting up with something or someone, who we are clearly not agreeable with, because there hasn't been, as the dictionary puts it 'any interference,' that requires communication—whether positive or negative. Where there is no communication, there is no knowledge or understanding. This equals no intimacy and eventually no marriage. When we say the vow, 'for worse,' I do not believe we have to tolerate bad attitudes, behaviour and not say anything.

Acceptance, on the other hand, was described in the dictionary as 'consent to receive; required with favour; agree to meet; pleasing and welcome.'

All of those descriptions come across to me as positive and, more importantly, refer to a communication that has to be present in order for agreement and consent to take place.

The other day Kevin made the breakfast and brought it upstairs to the bedroom, as he has done on numerous occasions, at weekends. Our 'Couple Connect' group had met the previous evening and we had discussed how much more we could all show our love to our spouses and to show how much we value each other. I was very grateful for my breakfast and the fact that he does this, without any prompting, every weekend morning and on his day off. However, later when I went downstairs, I couldn't help noticing that some of last night's washing up was still on the kitchen worktop waiting to be done. Now, my natural inclination when I prepare breakfast is to wash things up while I'm waiting for the kettle to boil for example. So, a thought came creeping into my mind, 'Why couldn't he have washed up while doing the breakfast?' 'Why has he left me to do 'all' the washing up? Why does he only do half the job?'

I gently made mention of this later that day and yes, it did cause a minor upset. He felt, understandably, that I didn't appreciate what he had done for me. I hadn't shown appreciation but criticism of him as a person. He felt put down. He was right about my tactless criticism, but after we'd discussed about how we both felt and how we can both make allowances for each other's mistakes, we came to an understanding and he accepted my apology for my rudeness and bad timing but also the essence behind the complaint. (Note that there is a difference between complaining and criticising!) We have agreed to a new suggestion of him washing up as soon as we are both dressed (and if he has seen it first!) and I have learnt to be more tactful. I could, however, have just ignored the whole situation and become more and more resentful towards Kevin, as I 'tolerated' this omission, but that wouldn't have been an honest representation of my true feelings. This is a fairly trivial example and I know that it is important to choose your arguments too. But let us nip things in the bud, when we can, to avoid misunderstandings and accept each other…for better, for worse!

There can be a fear of intimacy, a fear of rejection and some couples never open up to each other because of these fears and then just tolerate anything to remain in a relationship that suits them. That is not real love and therefore not the kind of meaningful relationship that God wants you or I to have. Such marriages are shallow and unfulfilling. These fears of rejection are rooted in loneliness, "if you really knew me, you would leave," or a fear of inadequacy, "if I can't fulfil your expectations," or a fear of losing control, "now that you know how I feel, you may use it to control me."

Adam and Eve sewed leaves together to cover up their awareness of sin and the shame they felt when they had been disobedient. They did this when they had broken their special relationship with God by rebelling against Him.

We cover or hide ourselves with emotional leaves in the things we say or do or think towards each other. This is ultimately destructive, bringing the worst into our marriages. How can we bring the 'better' and properly understand the 'worst' when it happens? Well, pray to Him who can see through us and through fig leaves (Proverbs 21:2 TPT) and better still pray together, if you can. This brings more intimacy and understanding into the relationship. That way, more of the 'better' or best occurs in our marriages, which is what God wants for us!

We have touched on communication as one of the keys to a better relationship which leads to understanding and acceptance, but also a better attitude towards one another.

The insightful and amusing author, Lysa Terkeurst, writes in her book, 'The Best Yes', about the potential for; 'THE UNRAVELING OF A MARRIAGE.' She describes how she is dealing with a sweater that she had got caught in her spiral notepad—the wire had caught a thread of wool and pulled a huge snag in it. She was in her car at the time and, in her haste, she made a quick decision and snipped the tangled thread. That was the end of a favourite sweater.

This story was to illustrate a situation that she found herself in, like many of us do in our marriages. She and her husband had a row just before they were to go out on a date and in front of the children. Feeling angry and humiliated, her husband announced that he didn't want to continue with the date. She felt the same but didn't voice it. She could see how, like her sweater, she could easily cut the threads. But she persevered, as she wrote, 'But we pushed through the resistance we both felt and eventually talked. Talking through the snags. The pulls. The things that threaten to unravel us. There is a delicate nature to marriage.... The unravelling can happen so quickly.'

To me, that was bringing her best into the relationship, into the marriage. She spoke of 'repairing the snags the right way' by admitting she was wrong and asking forgiveness. She continued to explain that the repair was 'tying a knot and tucking it back into the weave of our relationship fabric'.[v]

This 'tying of the knot' when we first get married is not just something that you do on your wedding day but every day. Recognising and accepting each other's weaknesses and encouraging one another's strengths—becoming one.

When you think about it, tying knots is quite a task in itself. Some of us remember helping our children learn how to tie their shoelaces—it takes some concentration! And all of us have at some time worn an apron, including my husband, fumbling to tie it behind our backs! It is so easy to give up. You need dexterity of mind and thumb, plus perseverance. Oh! And then there are those knots that happen—the worst times—which shouldn't have happened and you wonder why and how they have? String and jewellery come to mind and again it takes patient endurance to get through the task of unravelling those knots that get more complicated the less care and attention we give. In marriage, it is the knots of our attitude, fears and bad communication.

These worst areas of ourselves come into our marriages through our upbringing, our personalities and our gender. They are unavoidable and that is why we vow to accept each other through the worst as well as the better times!

We are different as men and women because God made us different, not only physically of course but our whole makeup. It is what causes the attraction in the first place. I believe God made us to think differently as men and women because it was His plan that we should 'complement' each other. In that way, with God's help, our love will grow.

'Her husband can trust her, and she will greatly enrich his life. She will not hinder him but help him all her life...Her husband praises her.' (Proverbs 31:11,12 &28 NLT)

In her book 'Feminine Appeal,' Carolyn Mahaney writes about, "our husband's particular sins, unique weaknesses, and even their idiosyncrasies are tailor-made for us. Likewise, our sins and weaknesses are custom-designed for them."
Thank God for our differing personalities. A couple of years ago, Kevin and I decided to set up a small group for married couples. The idea or concept was from an organisation in the United States, to encourage couples in their marriages. We had tried doing 'courses' with some success but many couples used to come up to us at the end of the evening and often comment, or noted on their feedback sheets, their need or desire to meet and chat with the other couples during the course, and not just at the beginning or end of the evening. We had always sold our courses on the basis of 'no group work!' However, we decided that we could meet more regularly at our home—a safe environment with ground rules of confidentiality, where couples could share, not only privately together, but with the group, their funny stories, their feelings about an agreed topic and differing opinions. 'Couple Connect' was formed in 2015.

As a group, we decided to look at the topic of personalities using the teachings of Maria and Florence Littauer.[vi]

It was a revelation to us all. I now understand why Kevin is a workaholic, always busying himself, needs quiet and is very thorough. I am, on the other hand, predisposed to putting loud music on or some kind of perceived 'noise' according to Kevin, while I do my chores. I am very easily distracted and can quite often just sit and relax knowing that I will get the job done eventually. We are both very emotional but I'm more dramatically so. Kevin wears his heart on his sleeve.

The personality analysis is nothing new. It goes back to those great Greek thinkers (around 400 BC) who philosophised about all things to do with life and the universe. It was Hippocrates who decided that what made people different in their thought patterns was caused by their differing body chemistry. A Greek physician called Galen (AD190) built on this concept and created what he described as the four Temperaments or personality types. These were based on an imbalance of certain bodily fluids like Sanguine-blood; Choleric-yellow bile; Melancholic-black bile and lastly Phlegmatic-phlegm. (I hope you are not eating a meal as you read this, particularly the last one!) The Phlegmatic description has me slightly retching at the sound of the word 'phlegm' but it is actually the other side to my personality and one that I fortunately share with Kevin. The author, Marita, describes us as peaceful, less driven and balanced people. However, where we differ is in our other personality types.

Kevin displays the characteristics of the melancholic. This does not mean that he gets easily depressed—it just means that he strives for perfection, believing that everything that he does matters and is worth doing extremely well. If things or people let him down, he could be more disappointed than the rest of us. My other 'type' is a sanguine hence the loud music and brightly coloured clothes that I tend to lean towards. Thank God for our phlegmatic tendency that gives us a 'meet in the middle' opportunity to appreciate our differences. I am happy to lose myself in the kitchen with the radio on while Kevin needs to concentrate on a focussed activity in a quieter room. I have learnt to use that time to enjoy my own company instead of resenting being on my own. Equally, I occasionally recognise Kevin's need to be affirmed in what he is doing or organising and listen to him quietly and attentively, however boring I might find it sometimes. For example, the other day he needed me to look at a job description and the possible accommodation that would come with it. Obviously, I was fairly interested because it affected me too, but it was Kevin's melancholic approach to everything that was so laborious and particular and opposite to my sanguine tendency to making snap decisions and getting on with the next exciting thing. I really had to concentrate and get into his way of thinking. It's this contrast that Kevin and I have to work out in our marriage. Over the years we have moulded to each other and even laughed at our different styles and approaches, according to our personality types; neither one of us being better or worse than the other but trying to bring the better of our differences and seeing how God can use us. (2 Corinthians 12:9)

There is a stereotype that I have heard frequently expressed, that is that men marry women hoping that they will stay the same whereas women tend to marry men hoping that they will change them. I'm not sure whether that is completely true but I guess, although many couples spend a significant amount of time in each other's company before they marry, they may still not discover the best or worst of their spouse until many years into the relationship. Then, of course, there are the unpredictable circumstances of life which may cause good or bad changes in our spouse's behaviour. Rather than focussing on the good or bad behaviours or personalities of our spouse—which Mandy has already covered—I just briefly want to mention character. I know that I probably have more annoying habits and behaviours than Mandy, and at times we have driven each other 'up the wall' with things that we are unlikely to change about each other, but I have always chosen to look for the better rather than the worse.

Mandy would probably say that she prefers our mature relationship whereas I would probably prefer the more care-free 'falling in love' heady days of our youth, but I am reminded of the fact that I fell in love—and I am still 'in-love' with her character. It's during those times of irritation or frustration of Mandy's negative traits that I look to draw on her beguiling qualities that drew me to be attracted to her in the first place. This is why I advocate looking for the better version of our spouse rather than looking to amass a catalogue of negatives. The Bible says 'love keeps no record of wrongs' 1 Corinthians 13:5 (NIV), and although the flawed version of me does subliminally keep a few of those wrongs in reserve during a heated but fleeting verbal exchange, I know that God had purpose in allowing me to vow 'for better, for worse' because He is crafting a better me and a better Mandy by knocking off our sharp corners and honing us to be better versions of ourselves. For it says in Proverbs 27:17 (NIV) 'As iron sharpens iron, so one man sharpens another'.

On 'The Marriage Course' and in their book 'The Marriage Book' by Nicky and Sila Lee, they use the phrase 'adapting their strides to the other.' This is a wonderful analogy.[vii]

A few summers ago, we actually had couples doing a three-legged race on our local beach in North Somerset, and we took photos to use on our website. It clearly illustrates the need to work together, even when one of us is at a different step to the other. We must be patient in those worse times especially when our husband or wife is struggling in a particular area of their lives. In Ezekiel 34:2-5, God reveals His displeasure when we do not help or care for the weak and ride roughshod, only thinking of our own selfish desires.

Our upbringing has an effect on our expectations of each other. What each believes and understands about marriage and what it should be like is according to our own parental model. We may believe that what our family did is the better way, so as a couple there has to be agreed rules as to who does what; who decides what, and who takes the lead on those things that have to be done such as managing the finances, doing the housework, cooking, maintaining the car, organising the holidays etc. How will you make the big decisions about where you will live? And how you spend your money? Who will hold the purse strings? Or do you have a joint account?

Some of these things seem trivial on the surface but they do have a deeper impact on daily living and certainly affect your attitude and behaviour towards one another. Having an understanding and appreciation of our different upbringings will allow us to see better ways to enhance our marriage relationship, and avoid or lessen those weaker or worse moments of frustration.

Kevin and I have often tended to take the roles that suit our personality and what we are better at doing. I have always enjoyed doing the cooking and baking. Cleaning the house as well as doing those tasks such as the washing-up, ironing, sewing and supermarket shopping fall on me mainly because I have more time. It also allows my creative flair to escape! Kevin, on the other hand, is more technical than me and observed his father when it comes to 'do-it-yourself' tasks. He learnt a fair amount as a teenager and being an engineer, has a natural thought process that likes to work things out to perfection! He also has an understanding and inclination towards maintaining the car and garden. However, we do help each other in all these tasks when required at various times.

There are some wonderful verses in the Bible that highlight the importance of our roles as husband and wife towards each other. They show how much we mean to God through our interactions in our marriage as we 'match our strides' to one another. Let us remember that we alone cannot make ourselves perfect for each other. We have to 'keep (our) eyes on Jesus, who both began and finished this race we're in.' (Hebrews 12:2 THE MESSAGE) 'Clear the path…so no one will trip and fall…Help each other out.'(Hebrews 12:13 THE MESSAGE)

I am always concerned for marriages when I hear couples speak of their spouses as their 'rock.' "Oh no!" I say, I am sure he or she is a lovely, supportive and altogether a wonderful person in your eyes, but do not allow a human being to share or replace the solidity of God's sure foundation for your relationships. As we have said earlier, we are not perfect and we will let each other down on numerous occasions. Only God can be the rock in our lives. (Deuteronomy 32:4) When we look to Christ and submit to His authority in our lives, we are then able to grasp what He wants for us as a married couple.

We cannot make each other better or perfect. We need the Perfecter of our lives to cleanse us and create in us a new heart—to beautify us and help us to see the beauty in each other.

Last year we decided to decorate a small room in our house. We could see the potential of what we wanted to ultimately achieve, but before we could start, it meant that we had to strip away all the old, wrinkled and blemished wallpaper. We had to wash it off. We took it back to its former, raw elegance and created a new room.

> *'Husbands must love your wives with the same love that Christ showed the church. He gave up his life for her to make her holy and clean, washed by baptism and God's word...to present to Himself... without spot or wrinkle or any other blemish (Ephesians 5:25-27 NLT)*

> *'In the same way, you wives must accept the authority of your husbands, even those who refuse to accept the Good News...they will be won over by your pure, godly behaviour. Don't be concerned about the outward beauty that depends on fancy hairstyles, expensive jewellery or beautiful clothes. You should be known for the beauty that comes from within...which is so precious to God' (1 Peter 3:1-4 NLT)*

Let us draw on the Holy Spirit's power to 'loving one another with tender hearts and humble minds' (1 Peter 3:8)—For better and for worse.

Let's Pray

1. Lord, help us to be 'the best' for our husband/wife. Help us to accept ourselves, as well as our spouse, in our weaknesses and theirs. Only you, Lord, can turn our weaknesses into a strength.
2. Thank you for our different personalities, our different upbringings and that you made us different as men and women. ('As Iron sharpens Iron…' Proverbs 27:17 NIV)
3. Remind us always to turn to You in prayer with those knots and tangles that threaten to unravel our marriages. ('Catch all the little foxes before they ruin the vineyard of your love...' Song of Solomon 2:15 NLT)
4. Thank you for being our Rock and sure foundation.

Chapter 4

For Richer for Poorer

'Lust for money brings trouble and nothing but trouble' (1 Timothy 6:10 THE MESSAGE)

'Don't store up treasures here on earth, where they can be eaten by moths and get rusty and where thieves break in and steal. Store your treasure in Heaven where they will never become moth eaten or rusty and where they will be safe from thieves. Where ever your treasure is, there your heart and thoughts will also be' (Matthew 6:19-21 NLT)

You are still standing at the Altar, or by the table in the Registrar's office. (Maybe you are in a garden or on the beach?) Wherever the marriage ceremony is being held, still gazing lovingly into each other's eyes when you say those words "for richer, for poorer." What are you thinking? Not a great deal—except how happy you are at this very moment and how nervous you feel. I know that is how I felt and like all couples, you hope you will be financially okay throughout your married life. Many couples don't get married until they believe they are able to afford the wedding. That is sad and a little short sighted, as we don't ever know what's around the corner. Hence the scriptural references at the beginning of this chapter. It is to help us to focus on what is our priority in life, apart from our husband or wife of course!

For many young couples today, there are compound issues for them to overcome that not all of us have, or will, or need to experience—such as the ridiculous and extortionate house prices that force couples into the prospect of renting for many years, with high rental costs and not being able to buy their own home in which to bring up their children. There is, as well, student debt for those who have tried to improve their education in order to get a better job, but that doesn't guarantee a higher income.

There is definitely a gap between rich and poor. So, let me ask you a question. Whether you are approaching the wedding or whether, like me, you are reflecting after the event; how do you feel about the definition of rich and poor? Is it about how much you own materially or just the income factor?

Is it how you spend your time and the people you spend your time with? Is it about your values or your monetary wealth?

We can all 'feel' poor at various times of our lives and it's important for some of you, as you step out as a couple together, to consider this and not assume it is going to be rosy and 'happy ever after'. I say 'feel' poor because of our different definitions—according to a blog by Tammy Skipper, who writes for A Biblical Marriage.com. She quotes from an article that says 'even the poorest five per cent of Americans are better off financially than two thirds of the entire world.' I think that quote applies to many of us in Western Europe too.[viii]

> *'The rich and the poor have one thing in common: The Lord God created each one.' (Proverbs 22:2 The Passion Translation-TPT)*

Kevin and I didn't consider ourselves either rich or poor when we got married. Both of us had steady incomes from our nine to five jobs and lived very frugally. We were products of our generation, so it wasn't unusual to not 'have it all' but at the same time, we knew we had more possessions for our home than our parents, and certainly our grandparents, had as newlyweds. I did not have a washing machine or a three-piece suite for a few years into our marriage. I had my mother-in-law's forty-year old 'New World' oven with eye-level grill and many handmade tables and chairs from my father-in-law's carpentry department at a local college for the disabled, where he worked. Our bed, occasional tables and all linen accessories were given as wedding presents and we bought our own refrigerator. Our car, an old Hillman Hunter, was Kevin's twenty-first birthday present from his parents. It didn't last long but left us with fond and amusing memories. We have never been able to afford a new car and, to be honest, wouldn't want to as they lose their value so quickly. It is all about decision making together as a couple, with God's wisdom and where you place your values with His influence in your lives…for richer, for poorer.

> *'But blessed are those who trust in the Lord and have made the Lord their hope and confidence. They are trees planted along a riverbank with roots that reach deep into the water. Such trees are not bothered by the heat or worried by long months of drought. Their leaves stay green, and they go right on producing delicious fruit' (Jeremiah17: 7-8 NLT)*

As unbelievers, when we first got married, we were both careful with what we had financially. Kevin has always been methodical, as I have previously mentioned about his melancholic personality—it has been and still is very useful! He would keep a budget book, keeping a close eye on our income and outgoings. He still does keep a budget spreadsheet and I have asked him to explain all about how we budget according to 'Christians against Poverty'—the CAP course, at the close of this chapter.

At this point, I think it is important to note that there is a difference between being good stewards of the money that God has provided by being careful, as against coming across as less than generous, penny pinching and overly worried about finances in general. Believing and remembering Whose money it actually is and how He really wants us to spend it, is a trustworthy attitude; We just need to be open to hearing Him and willing to obey—easier said than done—I say as one who struggles in this area. I am so glad that Kevin and I balance each other out, so to speak, with him being more able to spend money where he sees a need and me being cautious and reining him in in situations where we really don't need to 'waste' our small pot of earnings! In the Gospel of Luke, Jesus responds to a man who is jealous and overly worried about not getting the money he thinks is his from his brother. Jesus gently warns him of the dangers of greed and accumulation of wealth for selfish gain.

"Beware! Don't be greedy for what you don't have. Real life is not measured by how much we own" (Luke 12:15 NLT)

Praise God that He never judges us or condemns but warns and guides.

Kevin and I have always had a joint account. This doesn't always suit everyone and each couple must mutually agree how they are going to manage their finances. Some friends of ours have coined the phrase, "separate accounts but not secret accounts." It is always advisable to be open and honest about our spending habits even when we have separate accounts.

There is a danger that if one partner earns more money than the other, they may feel that they have more of a say as to how it is spent and this will undoubtedly lead to resentment and suspicion. It could also produce disinterest in each other's lives as they misunderstand the importance of what each brings into the house to create a home.

After the vows are spoken, there is the exchange of rings. It is during this section of the marriage ceremony that the words 'all I am I give to you, all I 'have' I 'share' with you.' This statement of intent really sets the standard of how much you honour and love one another. If you can share money, you can share everything else.

For Richer for Poorer

When we say 'for richer, for poorer', what we are really saying is that we are ready to go through the difficult, lean times of unemployment, less income, debt and long-term illness together, if and when they happen. Equally, when things go right for one of us, they go right for both of us. In marriage you have each other to comfort and encourage.

> *'For I (we) have learnt how to get along happily whether I (we) have much or little…I (we) have learnt the secret of living in every situation, whether it is with a full stomach or empty, with plenty or little.' (Italics mine) (Philippians 4:11-12 NLT)*

It is a wonderful thing when a couple can accept each other's weaknesses and disappointments and still go on loving and caring for each other. Kevin has always mused at the notion that he believes I have 'married down'. I always laugh at this because our thoughts are determined by how we view things and I definitely disagree and tell him off for saying so! Our financial backgrounds were quite different as we grew up. While Kevin was being driven around, by his dad, in a hired car every time they went on holiday because they didn't have a car of their own, my dad not only had his own car but a variety of them throughout my childhood. My mum also had her own car and we had a caravan, a boat and a large detached house. Kevin, however, was living in a terraced house in London before moving to a modest semi-detached house in Devon. I experienced private education in a convent school, while Kevin went along to the local comprehensive just down the road from me—long before we met! We started watching colour television in 1975 but 'poor' Kevin and his family were viewing television in black and white until much later in the seventies! Petty comparisons really but they can create a false sense of security or lack of it. There can also be an unhealthy expectation of your future husband or wife. In a blog post, highlighted in Preengaged.com, the writer looks at this vow with a number of considerations which would be good to refer to before we utter those less thought about words 'for richer, for poorer.'

It suggests you;

1) Consider the work ethic of the person you are about to marry, is it good?
2) Think about their trustworthiness in working hard at whatever you are both pursuing?
3) Prepare yourselves to live frugally if that is necessary. Could you live on a budget until you can afford what you have been used to?

4) Think about whether you should wait until you have enough money saved? If so, when is enough? (What I said earlier!)
5) And lastly (which took my attention to this particular blog in the first place). Are you prepared to leave your mother and father's house? In other words, are you ready to leave the lifestyle you have become accustomed to?

This last question has to be asked because of the 'leaving' and 'cleaving' aspect of the marriage ceremony and questions the expectations we might have, as we become a new unit.

'A man leaves his father and mother and is joined to his wife and the two are united into one'... (Genesis 2:24 NLT)

When we live at home with our parents, it is their role to meet our physical and emotional needs. As we grow and become independent, their role is to show us how to become less dependent and more able to give back to them, preparing us for our own roles as husbands and wives as well as parents, making our own decisions. Eventually, as a married person, our independence should be complete. We enter a new centre of gravity with our spouse; A new decision-making structure.

In the area of finance, this is especially important. There have to be clear and careful boundaries put in place with regard to our relationship with our parents and in-laws. That is to say, we don't cut ourselves off from them but rather connect in a new way as a couple. All decisions must be mutually agreed with our spouse's acknowledgement before making any decisions with our parents and in-laws.

It is common knowledge that many children need financial help from their parents at some time in their lives, even after they are married. Not only did we receive various furniture and equipment for the home, provided for us by our families, but my father was financially able to help us purchase our first washing machine, which we duly paid back in instalments. Purchases of that size, along with our first three-piece suite, I remember, left us with a pit in our stomachs. It took us along time to choose. We would go in and out of the store re-evaluating whether the one we had chosen really was the right one—best value and had all the bells and whistles we needed. When we bought our first refrigerator, Kevin cashed in his first pension plan.

It seems so final when you have to decide, "right we are going for this one!" and you announce it to the store assistant, who expects you to pay with your 'card' by the pressing of a few buttons— it is so quick— or you just 'wave' it in front of a card payment machine. In our case, we gingerly wrote out the amount in a chequebook and that was it—we felt we had signed our lives away. But a few days later, our new washing machine arrived and just as our friends and family said would happen, we found ourselves sitting in front of it, in the kitchen, watching every cycle of the wash click, turn and judder—we felt rich!

I don't think young couples today get quite so excited about appliances but they still need to 'leave' their parental home emotionally, psychologically as well as physically. Selwyn Hughes, in his book 'Marriage as God intended' considers the factors that come into play when one of the spouses looks back at the security and home comforts of their parents' home. The marriage relationship could easily become tense. When the wife still holds onto the emotional pull of her parents by listening more to their thoughts, advice and feelings than her husband, she creates insecurity and a belittling of her husband's authority. Equally, a husband who still comes under his parent's emotional control will find it difficult to maintain his role as head of his home. He will feel inadequate.

In the area of money and budgeting, the trust factor plays such an important part in the marriage relationship. When having to borrow money from our parents and in-laws, we would not only have to 'leave' our parents' influence but need to 'cleave' or be 'joined' together in our thoughts and decision making, as a couple, in order to be able to establish a united front towards them. In other words, creating access without allowing their control. We do not need a sense of dependence or to be in debt to anyone, including the extended family. Developing a healthy and harmonious relationship with our respective in-laws is the best way to enjoy a supportive, trusting relationship with our husband or wife.

'For richer, for poorer'...what does God expect of us as we say those vows to each other? He expects us to be a 'reflection' of His love. He poured out His love when He gave His life for us. If we are empty, how can we give to each other?

A husband is commanded to 'Go all out in your love for your wife exactly as Christ did for the church' (Ephesians 5:25 THE MESSAGE). His wife is to respond lovingly in submitting to his love and protection. This richness of love, this wealth of kindness is how we respond to one another. I will always remember my mother-in-law advising me when I married her son that marriage "is like a box, you only get out of it what you have put in."

For Richer for Poorer

'True humility and fear of the Lord leads to riches, honour and long life' (Proverbs 22:4 NLT)

In marriage, our relationship can become much more richly rewarding if we give of ourselves rather than just take what we can from the relationship. If we take and never give then we will be the poorer for it. In fact, I heard of an elderly couple who said they would only use the phrase 'give and receive' not 'take' because of the selfish implication. When we make selfless deposits every day towards our husband or wife, we effectively fill their emotional 'Love Bank.' We can then expect to be in credit for a 'richer' relationship.

Making a marriage work is costly and self-sacrificing. That is why, when we say the vow, 'for richer, for poorer', it is not that we have to put up with being poor or just 'cope' with being rich! It is about our heart attitude, towards our husband or wife, whether we are rich or poor. Kevin and I were very sad to hear of the divorce of our neighbours, many years ago when we first settled in the southwest of England. The wife had previously indicated that she worshipped money. She had to be making money and enjoyed a luxurious lifestyle, buying what she wanted, when she wanted. We both remember the look on her husband's face as she spoke to us over dinner one evening when they came to visit. We do not think they had ever really discussed this issue between them. When we happened to see the husband a few years later, he told us they were divorcing. They had clearly not understood this vow and the seriousness of it.

'Love can't be bought, love can't be sold- it is not to be found in the market place'. (Song of Songs 8: 7 THE MESSAGE)

This passage of scripture from the Message Bible sums up the attitudes of some couples today where they go into marriage believing they are going to 'get' all they want and expect from their spouses. When Mr or Mrs Right does not measure up, they give up and start looking for that illusive person who might, or they sometimes give up altogether. We should all look for the treasure within; that which is most valuable is freely given. Jesus said, "There is still one thing that you lack..." (Luke 18: 22 NLT) He was speaking to the rich young ruler who obeyed God religiously. He was looking into the young man's heart and soul but could see that he was unable to give of himself completely.

On another occasion, Jesus was sitting in the Temple court of women, where the treasury was located. It was made up of a number of boxes. There were seven for the Temple tax and six for the freewill offerings. There was an elderly woman who was very poor but she still gave 'two small copper coins.' Jesus remarked 'this poor widow has given more than all the rest of them combined. For they have given a little of what they didn't need, but she…has given everything she has' (Luke 21:3-4 NLT)

Do you lack anything in your marriage? Are you willing to bring your wealth of gifts into your relationship? Are you willing to bring everything you have, however little you think it is? As pointed out in the second chapter, in marriage, we are a team. We are joined together by God and we look to Him for our needs as a couple. We cannot put our faith in money the same way that we have faith in God. Only He can provide all we need at the right time.

It's not untypical in any marriage to find yourself with a different attitude to money than your spouse. For some couples the difference can be extreme, but for Mandy and I we have been broadly on the same page. On the whole, I describe Mandy as a 'natural saver' while I'm more of a natural spender. It's not that I prefer shopping or buying, it is just that I find it easier to spend money than Mandy does. For example, Mandy will quite happily visit three shops to get the best bargain whereas I will rather pay slightly more and save the time. Sometimes Mandy's cautiousness has allowed us to save money that we can then spend on the things we have patiently waited for. Whereas, my impulsiveness has prompted both of us to give, where we see a need. We have turned this 'difference' into a strength.

It would be very wrong to say here that we have got it all sorted, because we haven't. We have found certain principles for managing our finances have given us greater stability than some couples that struggle. Now I realise that for some reading this your circumstances might be very different from how ours have been and are currently. It may be that you have had to endure extreme hardship, or are comfortable, or both at different times in your marriage. All we can share is our story and how we have managed thus far. For us, we have gone through both tough times and modestly comfortable times, but I wouldn't ever have described us as 'rich' financially.

We have always had the principle of openness and honesty. There was a time, before we became Christians, when we worried about every single penny on our bank statement, but since we have realised that it's money that God has blessed us with, and we just loan it from Him, we have far fewer disagreements about it.

(1 Timothy 6:17-19 NLT) says 'Tell those who are rich in the world not to be proud and not to trust in their money, which will soon be gone. But their trust should be in the living

God, who richly gives us all we need for our enjoyment. Tell them to use their money to do good. They should be rich in good works and should give generously to those in need always being ready to share with others whatever God has given them. By doing this they will be storing up treasure as a good foundation for the future so that they may take hold of real life.'

I have been the one that has taken the role and responsibility of looking after the family finances, but we would both agree that the role is best suited to the one in the relationship with the best skill set for monitoring and checking our income and outgoings.

Our principles are;

- Don't live beyond your means. (Don't spend more per month than you have coming in. If you do this for a prolonged period you are on the road to ruin.) Try to work out a budget of how much you typically spend per month, against your total income. If you don't know what this is then one of you needs to do this and the other needs to be aware of spending boundaries.
- Avoid borrowing money for non-essentials. Make sure you are confident you can afford to pay back.

- Try to have safety margins in your budget so that if fluctuations in income occur, or that unexpected expenditure happens (emergencies, breakdowns, repairs etc.), you have the reserves to cover it.
- Don't buy without shopping around for the best deal.
- Have an overdraft facility on your bank account(s), but try to make sure never to use it.
- Use credit cards wisely! (if you can trust yourself not to spend beyond your means) but always pay the balance back in full and on time so that you never pay interest.
- Try not to think of income into the house as 'my' money or 'yours' but as 'our' money. Likewise, never think of bills or debts as mine or 'yours' but as 'ours'.
- Treat yourselves occasionally but don't let it become compulsive or addictive.
- Never use pay-day loan companies.
- Never gamble.
- Keep your finances confidential. Don't share this with people outside of your marriage, particularly with extended family or friends, lest they make

judgements or assumptions about your spending habits or what you can afford.

- Avoid waste. Don't buy something because it's in a sale, or if it is a 'bargain', if you don't need it. (This is particularly true of food that can go off.)
- Try to buy things that don't depreciate too quickly, so that you can sell them before they become worthless. (This is particularly true of cars.)
- Never make a financial commitment or lend money to someone else without involving your spouse in the decision.
- If your partner makes a purchasing mistake that either they or both of you regret, do not hold it against them or let it come between you.
- Never buy something from a cold-caller. If their product is 'that good', and they are genuine, they should be willing to either give you written information about it first, or allow time for you both to make the decision.
- Monitor your income and spending and don't assume everything is alright. Check statements and bills.
- Don't live in denial if your finances are in trouble or out of control. Seek help and advice from a

professional whom you trust. Don't put your head in the sand, hoping it will go away. It will get worse if you leave things.

- Investments. Earlier I listed gambling. Unfortunately, many savings and investment schemes are based on the stock market. In my view, the stock-market, is one of the biggest gambling casinos in the world, with both winners and losers. The world financial markets are very fluctuant and sensitive to geo-economics and politics. Business and stock appears to be based more on hypothetical worth rather than tangible value. For those of us who have pensions and long-term investments that are tied up in the stock market, we can only make speculative judgements based on our attitudes to risk. The jury is still out as to whether our generation, or subsequent ones, will have made wise choices in our investments. Being a cautious person myself, I have always tried to spread the risk rather than putting 'all our eggs in one basket!'

In the early years of our marriage we did very little formal budgeting. We lumped all our money into one joint bank account. As Mandy has already pointed out, having joint accounts may not suit everyone, but we found that it made us accountable to each other. Having one account sort of worked because we monitored it regularly and I kept a record of balances in a hand-written logbook. It was, however, very laborious to maintain, and it soon became apparent that we needed to have a separate joint account from which we paid our bills. I prided myself in never having had to pay any bank fees. We did once get charged a fee of £2.28 that later proved to be a mistake on the bank's part! However, in more recent years we have adopted a three accounts system that I monitor on a computer spread-sheet.

I decided to do this after Mandy and I attended a Christians Against Poverty (CAP) course.[ix] One doesn't need to be in poverty to attend one of these, and I would highly recommend it as a way of getting to grips with money as a married couple or individual. We discovered that it enabled us to be able to plan ahead better. In our first year, after the course, we discovered that it gave us the confidence to go on two annual holidays rather than one because we had made provision for it. Equally, we have heard testimony of others that have been in debt whom have managed to become debt-free by adopting the strategies that CAP suggest.

We have modified their suggestions to make a comprehensive system for ourselves. The CAP money course can explain the basic principles far better than we can, but the following is a summary of what we do.

Simply put, we have one account where all income goes in. What comes out of this account is our mortgage, utility bills, regular monthly outgoings and payments to two other accounts.

The second account, which we shall call the 'Cash' account, receives monthly money from the first. This sum is based on an average of monthly, and relatively predictable amounts, we expect to pay on food, cleaning and other supermarket type goods. Out of this account also comes petrol and train fares etc. For those that struggle with curbing their spending, this is literally an account from which cash or 'real' money is spent so that they can see how much they have left to spend in any week.

The third account also receives money from the first account monthly and is loosely called a 'Savings' account. This is where money is put aside for items we will need to pay for, either annually or in the future. This includes things like road tax, car repairs, home maintenance, annual insurance, birthdays, Christmas, and ideally holidays and luxury items for the home, if there is sufficient left. The luxury non-essential items are your 'disposable' income, if you have any. The other 'savings' are things that you will have to pay for and will need to have in place rather than them come as a surprise. In truth, this is a rather abridged version of what we do as we have multiple columns in our spreadsheet so that we can monitor imaginary money 'pots' within the third account so that we can review whether the money will build up in time for the individual categories of annual outgoings.

I realise that all this monitoring and predicting income and outgoings is a little dull and time consuming, but if it gives you better visibility, so that you can plan your future a little more predictably, it will reduce the amount of stress and arguing that occurs in so many 'just about managing to get by' family units.

I am acutely aware that circumstances can change, and income can vary wildly, particularly for those on zero-hours contracts, variable hours, self-employed, the birth of children, illness and through unemployment. But getting control of spending and having a better 'idea' of how things are going can only be a good thing. I personally have been made redundant three times in my career and Mandy has had many jobs with variable income, but somehow God has blessed us by keeping us out of the danger zone.

Let's Pray

1. Thankyou Lord that You are our provider; that you will never leave us or forsake us and we can trust You if we seek Your kingdom first.
2. Help us Lord to remember that all we have has been given to us by You and not of our own doing. Thank You for all our financial blessings. Help us to not be greedy or selfish but to bless others.
3. Help us to submit to one another in our finances. "All that I have I share with you" will be my vow (or I have made this vow). May we become 'one' in all that we own, so that money does not divide us.
4. Ask God for a heart of contentment—whether you have much or little — 'abased or abound!'

Chapter 5

In Sickness and in Health

'A cheerful heart is good medicine, but a broken spirit saps a person's strength' (Proverbs 17:22 NLT)

We have met a few exceptions, but the vast majority of couples commit to this vow when they are both healthy. I am humbled by those who choose to marry when the partner they love is either terminally ill, disabled, or when there are unusually difficult challenges beyond the challenge of learning to live and think as a couple, rather than as an individual.

For the majority, when considering sickness, I wonder how many might think that marriage is untenable if their partner's personality changes due to a mental health problem, or the permanent inability to communicate, or do things together as a result of a physical disability. I guess this is why the vows are sometimes called 'solemn vows' because they are not to be entered into without considered thought.

At the time of writing, I am coming to the end of an illness that has lasted for over nine years. Mandy suggested that I write things from my perspective for this chapter, but in many ways, this is not about the illness that I have had to endure, but rather the affect that it has had on our marriage.

I guess that in the haze of our love for each other, particularly as we set out on the journey of marriage, we both would have considered the 'in sickness' vow little more than fleetingly, with a hope that that would never be part of our experience. Indeed, like almost everybody, we both hope that it won't feature again in the future, but life doesn't always work out quite the way romantic novels portray. I am sure that for some, illness, accident, disease, and even bereavement of a spouse, can be far worse than what we have experienced thus far, but hopefully you can read behind the sentiment of my experience.

I would like to point out, without going into a full personal medical history, that largely we were both physically fit and completely healthy going into marriage, despite a spot of hay fever on my side and both having to wear glasses. Since getting married, probably between the two of us, I seem to have experienced the most heath issues and investigations along the way. I am truly grateful for Mandy's support and God's help in weathering these storms.

Now, for the last few years I have been suffering from something I understand to be called Chronic Headache or Migrainous Vertigo. The World Health Organisation (W.H.O.) lists migraine as one of the top 12 most debilitating conditions. I don't know how they measure this, and I certainly don't want to compare the suffering to that of many pretty nasty diseases and conditions I have seen others with, but I can tell you it is very debilitating. I'm not talking here about cluster headaches or the occasional migraine where one has to go into a darkened room for a few hours or days, but a persistent chronic background headache that has been noticeable—in varying degrees of severity—from the moment I awake to the moment I fall asleep. This, combined with fatigue, causes giddiness, dizziness and extreme vertigo. When it has been particularly bad, I experience loss of balance with sudden and unexpected giddy turns that have caused me to fall to the floor with, what feels like blood rushing to my head, and a concussed feeling like someone has just hit me over the head with a baseball bat. At worst, when not treated properly by the medics, I needed a walking stick to help me walk in a straight line. I remember sitting, whilst watching my oldest son's graduation ceremony, when my head felt so bad that I could barely support the weight of my head on my shoulders.

Aside from the initial fear that this might be something life threatening, and the near endless series of hospital appointments, test scans and more tests, one of the worst aspects was not getting a proper diagnosis and therefore not being able to find a suitable treatment. I saw various specialist consultant doctors but none that could provide me with any hope of beating the problem. Eventually I found one in Kent who is widely acknowledged as Europe's top specialist in the field of balance and neurological related disorders. He started me on a very strict diet and a series of different types of pills to try and get some equilibrium. I had never met anyone with a similar condition and still haven't to this day. During the early years of this condition I felt completely isolated, with no knowledge of whether I would ever get my old life back. It affected the food I was able to enjoy, where I felt safe to go on my own—in case of an episode, my work, my social life, the ability to be around loud music or bright-lights and my ability to drive.

Another aspect of the illness that was hard to come to terms with, was others' perception of it. On the face of it, and for the most part, there weren't any visible symptoms. I would occasionally get strange looks from acquaintances and friends.

Did they think I was just faking it or making a fuss about my strange diet? My lack of tolerance to bright-lights and loud noise was another oddity— after all I wasn't disabled and didn't have my arm in a sling! As a Christian, I have had many people pray for me, including the 'laying on of hands.' This has been very encouraging in terms of emotional support, but when prayer hasn't resulted in the immediate cessation of symptoms, I've shared in their disappointment and at times I would feel as though I failed them or even felt guilty for asking them to pray again. This is wrong thinking—I know!

During a large part of those years it was also particularly hard to function as the drugs I was being given to numb the symptoms, caused tiredness and more worryingly, a loss of memory and alertness. To make matters worse, I had also accumulated some other physical problems—that I don't need to go into—all coinciding with the beginning of the empty nest at home.

Our sons had now permanently left the family home to start their careers in London. Mandy and I had thought we could just ease ourselves into the new life of being just the two of us again. We dreamed of new adventures, romantic times together and being able to make plans. Instead, I was feeling; unwell, exhausted, lethargic, frustrated and emasculated. How could I, the male leader in our relationship take charge, offer security and do simple things like drive the car when I was not even sure whether I would collapse on the short journey to work, or was at times, hanging onto the edge of my desk at work with all my strength to stop me falling off the chair? Why am I telling you all this? The point is that Mandy and I never planned for this and obviously it's not something we would have chosen. Who would? The future appears uncertain for my health, for Mandy's health and potentially all of us as we get older but in God it is certain.

Although it appeared that prayers were not being answered, Praise God, He had started the healing process and things are improving for me as the years roll on. Mandy has been a tremendous support to me during this time, tackling difficult dietary plans—that seemed to make no difference at all, as it turns out—and ferrying me to the train station for work, doing all the driving, which I used to do a lot of, escorting me to umpteen hospital appointments, besides putting up with the emotional roller coaster of not knowing from one day to the next how able I feel 'to do' things. I also have the concern about the feelings of distress she must be experiencing through watching me struggle during bad turns and the fact that some of the medications have caused me to seem distant, forgetful and even a little aggressive in my reactions. I also have to ask myself the question, had she been the one with the chronic symptoms, would I have been able to offer the practical support and optimistic encouragement she has afforded me through this time?

I am aware that she also has her own physical health battles to fight and realise that I may also need to step up to the plate in other areas of our life should her health deteriorate with age. Having said all of that, with the help of God, I think we have fared pretty well to keep the marriage ministry—our vision for us—and our love for each other just as strong as it's ever been, through the tough as well as the good times.

I asked Kevin to write this chapter from his perspective but he thought I ought to say a few words!

I came across a very interesting article that looked at the psychology of health (both good and bad) in couples and how we can affect each other. This article pointed out that although our families, friends and our own personal goals and values have an effect on our lifestyles, our loved ones do have an influence on our emotional and physical wellbeing. In the article's description, it noted that we tend to have relationships with others of similar backgrounds, behaviours and ways of thinking.[x] So if our husband or wife is a smoker, for example, or enjoys unhealthy food like takeaways etc. and/or drinks alcohol regularly, then there will be a tendency to join in. In fact, when a couple marry, their behaviour becomes even more alike—which we know happens—as God has joined them together in body, mind and spirit. Sadly, we also know that when God is disregarded in that 'joining,' then bad habits can move us away from Godly lifestyles. The article went on to explain how the quality of your marital relationship can affect your medical status. Where there is more hostility in a marriage, there is likely to be more signs of coronary artery disease. And where there is a form of control and dominance from either the husband or wife, a similar medical condition can occur than for those in warmer, more egalitarian relationships.

How can we improve the health of our marriages and thereby improve the health and well-being of our spouse at the same time? St. Paul, asks, 'Are your hearts tender and sympathetic?' (Philippians 2:1 NLT) He continues in verse 4, 'Don't think only about your own affairs (*interests*) but be interested in others too and what they are doing.' (my paraphrase in italics)

Being interested and concerned, looking out for the well-being of our spouse by the way we do things should be obvious but maybe, because we are living in such close proximity, we overlook our immediate responsibility. In the Message Bible translation, it simply puts it this way in verse four. 'Forget yourselves long enough to lend a helping hand.'

When we say that vow, 'in sickness and in health', do we honestly consider the implications of those words and the responsibility that they carry if the care giving falls to us? Generally, I think we don't; we live in hope that it will not happen to us.

For over twenty years, I had the opportunity and privilege to be a 'Relief Carer', or as I became latterly known, as a 'Community support worker' for sufferers of Dementia and their carers or loved ones. Being a part of this work enabled me to become very close to those I was assigned to help and sometimes I felt like they included me as a member of their family. I have to say that the male 'carers' either a son or husband, found it most awkward to deal with looking after their mum or wife. But my overriding observation was the devotion given in such difficult circumstances, particularly for husbands and wives. As children we kind of expect to help our aging parents. However, caring for a spouse with a disease like dementia, can really challenge the marriage relationship; various forms of dementia can bring about emotional as well as physical changes. I have observed husbands and wives not recognising their spouses and treating them like strangers or siblings. A most troubling situation is when a husband or wife with this illness becomes suspicious and accuses their caring spouse of things they haven't done. (Like having an affair when they had just popped out to get the groceries!) These changes cause more stress than the physical ones of immobility and incontinence but overall one is seeing your husband or wife slowly dying before your eyes and not be able to do anything about it except to care the best you can. This is such a testing to this vow.

However, this is our duty as a husband; this is our duty as a wife. It is what we signed up for if this possibility arose. Do we love this person, who we are standing next to, saying this vow to, enough? It saddens me to hear of cases where a mother is caring for a disabled child—alone. The husband couldn't cope and walked out. Sometimes, but less often, the wife walks out. I also understand that we all have our own thresholds of pain and discomfort and I have no right to point a finger and judge the heart and mind of another human being—only God can do that. However, it still saddens me, as I believe the vow encompasses the well-being or otherwise of our family unit, including our offspring. Quite often, it is down to that common illness of bad communication. It will 'seep' like a poison into our relationship, infecting our thought processes, becoming a contagious habit of mistrust and disrespect and slowly we believe the virus of lies that destroy the love we once had. Sometimes, it is just a simple misunderstanding that isn't communicated because there is no inner knowledge and appreciation of each other.

In this same article by Rebecca Webber, she relates a story about a couple where the guy leaves his wife after two years as she had contracted Hodkins Lymphoma. "I didn't know how to tell him what I wanted, and he didn't know how to ask", she said.

Kevin started this chapter with the question of how we should be looking at the health of our marriages. How we communicate can have devastating consequences on our health and in turn affect our marriages; these are sadly avoidable.

In Psalm 141:3 King David asks, 'God give me grace to guard my lips from speaking what is wrong'. (TPT) And in the book of James, he also reminds us of the tongue's 'uncontrollable evil, full of deadly poison,' (verse 8 NLT)

Only a few hurtful words, even if said in jest, can be very damaging to our long-term health and, in turn, can affect our moods—the way we feel about ourselves and each other and the choices we make and whether to stay or to leave!

'Respond gently when you are confronted and you'll defuse the rage of another. Responding with sharp, cutting words will only make it worse'. (Proverbs 15:1 TPT)

'A cheerful heart puts a smile on your face, but a broken heart leads to depression' (Verse 13) and 'Everything seems to go wrong when you feel weak and depressed. But when you choose to be cheerful, every day will bring you more and more joy and fullness.' (Verse 15)

These wise words from King Solomon in his book of Proverbs speak so clearly of the importance of our individual attitudes and how we communicate them in our relationships. When we vow to keep each other 'in sickness and in health', we must consider our communication as key—with a large dose of humour a necessity.

Let's Pray

1. Ask the Holy Spirit to 'Search me and know my heart, test me and know my anxious thoughts. See if there is any offensive way in me…' (Psalm 139:23,24 NIV) Let us check our own heart health as we are about to say these

vows or from today in our own marriage - we can start afresh. 'His compassions never fail. They are new every morning' (Lamentations 3:22, 23 NIV).

2. Give thanks in all circumstances. For the health you have and the healing that God is bringing to your body, mind and spirit. 'and by His wounds, we are healed' (Isaiah 53:5 NIV)
3. For God's strength to get you through each day, for one another. 'The joy of the Lord is your strength' (Nehemiah 8:10 NIV)
4. For perseverance. Do not give up on God for healing; for the destiny and plan He has for you alone and as a couple. Ask, seek and knock without ceasing and be joyful always.

Chapter 6

To Love and To Cherish

'Be good wives to your husbands, responsive to their needs. Be good husbands to your wives. Honour them, delight in them.' (1 Peter 3:1,7 THE MESSAGE)

I want to take you right back to when you were first dating your husband or wife. I'm talking here about the time before your wedding day—the time when you made the decision to marry.

I'm hoping here that you weren't coerced or pressured, by your partner—or anyone else for that matter—to marry, but hopefully it was a time when you felt you had a deep connection and a deep conviction to spend the rest of your life with this person. Now, we have met a small number of young women, (sorry to be so gender specific!), that are more in love with the idea of getting married, (i.e. the romance and attention of the wedding day) rather than focussing on the 'tiny-bit' afterwards which is for the rest of their lives.

I want to bring things right back to basics. When you were in pursuit of your husband or wife you probably made it a priority to cherish them. You probably didn't speak to them in a harsh tone of voice. You wouldn't have put them down in front of your friends and you probably made space for them in your busy life. You almost certainly made time for them to love you back whether this was by dating, by phone or by the written word. Most likely your words would have been affirming and encouraging. There would have been an attitude of gratitude.

Can I ask a challenging question? This comes from a standing point of familiarity and possibly taking the other person for granted. How successful do you think you might have been in romancing and winning your partner's affections, if you had performed any dishonouring behaviour?

One of the ways I cherished Mandy when we first started dating, was with the amount of quality time I spent with her. It would be inaccurate to say that when I was young I had more spare time than I do now. At the time I was at College and then at University when it was a real struggle to manage my studies and travel back and forth most weekends from Surrey University to Salisbury, where Mandy was studying her nursing course. It would also be wrong to assume that I had my mind focussed wholly on my college whilst present there!

I cherished Mandy by having her in my thoughts frequently. You could put this down to being 'in-love' but I would say it was cherishing, because her interests, and helping her reach her dreams, as well as her general 'well-being' were foremost in my mind. Now, I recognise that for many guys sex occupies their minds for much of their 'formative' years but 'True Love' is always other person focussed rather than looking to meet one's physical needs. What do I mean by cherishing her with quality time? When we went out on a date, I listened to her with my heart as well as with my ears. I valued her thoughts and her opinions. I desired to share her world through the lens of her imagination. I wanted to step inside her world as she perceived it. I also wanted to gaze into her eyes and upon her innermost soul.

"But what of today?" I hear you cry, "when you have learned of most of her life stories and understood her opinions and try to guess from her expressions what she might be thinking?" Well, the attitude to listening should be just the same. I almost wrote 'the task' should be just the same, but that's the point, it shouldn't be an effort to listen; not a check box to be ticked. For intimacy to be maintained, there must be a genuine connection. Really connecting doesn't solely depend on sharing the same ideas, enjoying the same things and even agreeing with each other all the time. Connecting seems to be more about actively investing in time with each other. It means being fully present, engaged with and open to sharing experiences with our partner, even when the activity or event we are sharing is more enjoyable for them than us. I have to ask myself the question, when I was dating Mandy, did I ignore her opinions? Did I 'peel' myself away from the TV or computer? Well, the honest truth is that personal computers weren't in the picture then and I don't remember my TV viewing habits but I'm guessing that I would have been pro-active in my communication and less 'self' absorbed with what I was watching. Going back to the early days, how successful would I have been in creating a desire within Mandy to want to marry, or at least want to keep dating me, had I deployed sarcasm and criticism as my main stay of communication? When I say sarcasm, I'm not talking about friendly teasing but those cutting jokes that have a thread of veiled "what I really think about the person" in them. I'm pretty sure those things would have worked against me in the personality stakes.

I'm not so unrealistic as to suggest that as life changes we don't change. Our relationships do mature. The relationship is different from the boy meets girl scenario, but I am trying to highlight our negative attitudes that can so easily creep in over the passage of time. Quite a big issue for men, is what sort of work life they have (but this is by no means exclusive). For many, a career or job is a large part of a persons' identity, particularly as it occupies a large part of our time. In a move away from the hunter-gatherer instinct, men in the modern world, most often see earning a living and providing for their family as still being an important part of their role. Of course, many women provide a substantial part of the family income but during child bearing years, it is still the man that is mainly relied upon. It's all about setting appropriate boundaries. What is an appropriate balance? Is working hard to provide an income for a family bad? No, of course not, but if the pursuit of money to buy things becomes so consuming and absorbing that it causes pressures and friction, and ultimately damage to the family, then what purpose has it served? You know, I've never heard of anyone on their death bed that has expressed regret about wanting to have spent more time in the office or doing overtime but I've heard of quite a few that wished they had worked harder at their relationships and regret marriages that failed. I've also never met anyone who entered into marriage with the sole purpose of planning to wreck their partner's life. So where does it often go wrong? Well, of course, there is not one answer to this and I've often met many people that feel they have just been unlucky in marrying the wrong person. In some cases that may be true and I'm not judging that person or their relationship. However, from counselling struggling couples over the years, we have found marital breakdowns are more often a result of a gradual decay in the relationship over a prolonged period. Lack of good communication and/or not honouring our spouse is a cause of such decay.

Wrong priorities aren't just limited to putting a job or career before our wife or husband. Over-committing ourselves to other projects or people outside the house, including over-committing to leisure pursuits or the pursuit of possessions, can cause damage to a relationship. This is made all the more damaging if one half of the partnership has set very different goals or priorities to the other. We've also met quite a few couples along the way that fell into to the trap of living for and worshipping their children. Now don't get me wrong, children are a gift and there are many fabulous families, but it seems that many couples that reach the 'empty nest' season of their marriage had no vision or plan for what they wanted to do when the children have left the parental home. They wake up one morning, next to their husband or wife, having expended all their time, energy and devotion to their children and they find they are married to a stranger. Often, there is a dis-connect and an emptiness. This void is often filled with separate activities that keep the couple apart and with separate friends, sprinkled with occasional escapism together. The years of niggles about differences of how the children were disciplined and the lack of being valued as a husband or wife, rather than a father or mother, have left the couple battle weary. They exist as a couple either; walking on 'egg shells' trying to avoid the next conflict or without purpose, simply living together but with no determination to breathe life back into the marriage. Remember you made your vows to each other not to the children!

Having read, or listened to all this, you might be thinking that actually as a couple you are not doing too badly, or that you don't want this to happen to you, or worse still that you have become one of those couples that have drifted apart. Well, thankfully there are many tools and resources available that can help put you back on track.

One of the best ways to cherish your marriage is by investing time in it. Many couples have found it really helpful to attend a marriage enrichment course, marriage retreat or marriage intensive. This is certainly something we would recommend, having personally attended a few ourselves and led many such programmes and seminars. We would say this needs to be an ongoing commitment rather than a one off event, that kind of helps for a while, but is soon forgotten.

(Examples of how you can do this practically are given in the Appendix A.2)

What about the day to day? We can cherish our spouse by showing them our appreciation. If we were to announce to our partner that from this point on we intend to show more appreciation, it's most likely going to be met with disbelief and mistrust! In my view, the best appreciation is often unexpected. Heartfelt appreciation, where you can genuinely detail what you are thankful for, is useful in filling up the other person's emotional love tank. Regular appreciation is generally welcomed but needs to be communicated with different words rather than cited like a robotic script. Where regular appreciation has been absent from a marriage for a prolonged time, it needs to be introduced gradually to build trust. Verbal appreciation works well with a hug or a kiss on the cheek but a letter or note written by hand can be equally effective. Texts can be affirming but do not always arrive when you send them or can be often disregarded amidst the noise of social media.

If we are out of the habit of showing our appreciation, because we have taken our partner for granted, we may need to actively seek out what we are grateful for. This is often an act of the will and may feel slightly unnatural or fake at first, but we need to persevere for some time before it seems normal. You may feel that you already appreciate your partner, but unless you put those thoughts into words, your loved one is unlikely to have read your mind!

A sense of feeling there is not much to appreciate in your partner may stem from a lack of appreciation for who you are or what you do. Starting this process of sacrificially looking for the small blessings in your partner will eventually lead to discovering bigger blessings. In my estimation, it would be unusual if it were not reciprocated at least within a few months of earnest effort.

Ignoring or disregarding your spouse's opinion can have a massively negative affect on their self-image or confidence. This is heightened further if their parents ignored or disregarded their views when they were growing up. It may well be that you already think you know what they are going to say before they say it, but if they are habitually ignored, it will often lead to them closing down and to rarely open up to share. The danger of this kind of dishonouring is that they may choose to open up to a member of the opposite sex who is willing to listen. Over a period of time, this can lead to an unplanned affair.

Putting in-laws down or treating other relatives as unimportant can be majorly dishonouring. We've all heard jokes about mothers-in-law and how stereotypically they don't easily get along with their sons-in-law. But the reality is that in most families, there will be an element of disagreement brought to bear caused by different values, faith, culture, politics, class, tradition and expectations. In a sense when we marry someone we are also adopting their heritage and their family into the package—warts and all! In fact, we may not have fully grasped the positive or negative character traits, the frailty or the dysfunction of our in-laws or how their interdependence or dependence will affect us, and how that may change as we all grow in age and experience together. Generally, a child will have a bond with their parent(s), grandparent(s), sibling(s) or adoptive family as they grow up.

In a young marriage, where both husband and wife are brought together in matrimony while their parents are still alive, the traditional Christian wedding ceremony will be a symbolic act. The vicar or minister will typically ask the Father of the Bride whether they will give their daughter away. This symbolism is deliberate. In a sense, as the wedding ceremony is a public declaration that both 'his' and 'her' families are accepting and in agreement of the union. They will generally be asked to promise that they will do everything they can to support and help the couple, as the couple journey their way through life together. The ceremony also marks a new centre of gravity for the couple. They are now a new family unit. The difficulty occurs in the degree to which the in-laws are involved with the new family unit; too much and they can stifle the growing independence that the couple need to establish. They need to be a two, united as a one, rather than just a subset of the original families; too little and they can feel unsupported.

It is for the couple to agree together the level to which they plan to visit and communicate with their own parents and in-laws. The dishonouring happens when the husband or wife may deliberately make no effort or be unable to achieve a harmonious relationship with their in-laws. This is less of a problem when the spouse understands why the relationship with the in-law(s) is strained or difficult, but more awkward when there is a miss-match of values aligning within the new family unit.

There is no easy answer to the problem of difficult relationships within the wider family but we have found that having agreed boundaries has been useful in setting appropriate levels of communication. In the chapter 'For Richer, for Poorer,' Mandy looked at the difficulties that can arise in regard to our finances when the wider family interfere or just get involved.

Manipulation, when extreme, is a form of abuse. For many marriages this does not elevate to control by physical harm or emotional blackmail, but it is definitely dishonouring, however subtle. Manipulation is making or coercing your partner to do something against their choice or preference. It usually has a seed of fear in it. Any manipulation that involves making your spouse do or think something ungodly, or benefits only the manipulator is dishonouring. Broadly speaking, we can think of dishonouring as the opposite of cherishing.

So, how can we honour, that is to cherish, our spouse spiritually? We can do this by avoiding sins that will taint our husband or wife's character. We can cherish them by praying for them—with or without their knowledge. We can pray with them affirming and agreeing with their prayers. When we are truly connecting with their deepest needs and desires, we will know the prayers and desires of their heart before they utter them.

One area of connection that definitely needs to be spiritually honouring is our sexual union. It probably goes without saying but the marriage bed needs to be pure. A one-flesh union needs to be observed with both our bodies and our minds. Fantasizing about someone else, albeit with someone like a film character or porn image whilst making love to your spouse is still dishonouring to their spirit even if they are unaware of it; it's a deception. When we promise to give ourselves to our partner on our wedding day, we are not to withhold ourselves sexually either in the early days of marriage or through the years. Our bodies are no longer our own. They are to be shared as a gift to our spouse. (1 Corinthians 7:3-5). Much hurt can be caused in a marriage where sex is frequently withheld and when there is no legitimate reason for doing so. Men will often feel a deeper emotional and spiritual connection after 'making love' whereas for women it is often the other way around. They need to feel the emotional connection in order to partake in the 'love making' act in the first place. This is particularly true in marriage where sex is more often love focussed rather than lust focussed. For these reasons when a wife promises to make love to her husband at a time in the future, and then retracts that promise unreasonably, it can feel like a rejection. Similarly, if flirtatious advances are made by either spouse and are re-buffed too many times, the intimacy is dishonoured by a lack of trust, making it difficult for the rejected partner to make themselves vulnerable again.

We certainly don't cherish but rather dishonour our partner's faith by how we compare our faith to theirs. Although a couple can be sharing the same religious faith, their faith in God is always an individual, personal experience. Invariably, in the Christian faith, peoples' understanding and perception of their personal relationship with Jesus will vary wildly. There should be no reason to suppose the understanding and perception would be any different just because we are married. This is certainly true for Mandy and myself, even though we came to faith on exactly the same day over 30 years ago. Although our Christian education and our exposure to teaching and doctrine have broadly been the same, through attending the same churches, our experience of our faith and our comprehension and interpretation of biblical truth are coloured by the people we work with and communicate with from day to day. I would have to say, that I am slightly envious of the amount of nurturing and scriptural knowledge Mandy has acquired through years of regular attendance at a weekly ladies' Bible group. For me, work commitments have hindered a similar growth, but in other ways, I have benefitted from a period of a few years studying part time at a theological college. I would say that Mandy has a greater knowledge of the bible than me, but it would be very wrong to assume that my day-to-day conversations with God were any less valid. As a couple, we need to honour and cherish each other's spiritual experience. Our prayers, belief, and thoughts may be organised in our heads differently, but our different perspectives and our Holy Spirit connection needs to be encouraged rather than judged by our own reality.

Aside from sexual intimacy, physical honouring can be very subtle. Holding your partners hand can be very re-assuring. We have discovered that for men, when a wife holds her husband's hand, it can say to him that she wants to be vulnerable, she wants to be his, and she feels close to him. As a woman's need is often for that of security, when a husband holds his wife's hand it says, he wants to take care of her. There is another dimension particularly when walking hand in hand in public, that the husband is saying, "She is my proud possession. She is mine and hands off!" There is also a sense of the husband taking leadership. Drawing his wife along the path they have chosen to walk together.

For the first few years of our marriage I had been completely unaware that Mandy felt that I was holding her hand all wrong. There was the usual tussle of different heights, arm lengths, and hand size creating difficulties in getting a comfortable position walking side by side, but apart from that was the fact that Mandy always felt that my grip was a little limp. I had always been led to believe that the female hand was delicate and had always adopted a gentle hold so as not to crush her hand. But for Mandy, what she wanted was my firm grip. She wanted to feel held tightly. For her my tighter grip affirmed her desire to be protected and led by her 'knight in shining armour.' Much the same can be said for the arm around the waist, although this tends to be more casual. It is the husband who scoops up his wife and gently persuades her along—much like a romantic dance. The wife's arm around his waist is more of a, "I want to be yours" rather than a pushing of the husband. The wife should never lead the walk—or at least that is our view—other couples may adopt a different stance.

Then there is the etiquette of door opening; something that on occasion, I confess I still forget. In our politically correct world—which the feminist movement has had a hand in creating—it is not always assumed that the men should always be the first to open doors for women. Apparently, some women interpret chivalry as belittling. In our more traditional marriage, Mandy feels more of 'a lady' and me more of a 'gentleman' if I anticipate the opening of doors for her as my princess. The act of me being 'fully present' and ready to clear the way for her, gives honour to her. It also serves to remind me of her need to be physically preserved. This is particularly true for Mandy as she has a weakness in her wrists. It probably goes without saying but for the husband to help his wife put her coat on or carrying shopping can present similar serving and cherishing opportunities.

The way we dress, when married, needs to be reviewed in the light of being one entity rather than two individuals. That's not to say that we need to lose our identity when married, but we need to be respectful. This is something that has to be mutually agreed. For example, a husband might be okay with his wife wearing a low-cut top or a short shirt, but he might feel less comfortable taking his wife, dressed sexily, into a context where other men are 'eyeing her up.' Some men might want other males to feel envious of what he has, but call me old-fashioned, modesty seems more appropriate when we have found our mate for life. The question is, who is she dressing up for—herself, her husband or to attract the attention of other men? Generally, it's somewhat different the other way around. A husband or wife that dresses smartly or pays attention to their appearance, when with their spouse is saying to their husband or wife, 'I care enough to want to look tidy for you.' However, the attitude that says, 'I can't be bothered to dress the way I did when we first met' shows a lack of priority 'to value' the attraction we had when we first became acquainted. The same applies to personal hygiene. It's really important for husbands to affirm their wife's body image as they age. It's a fact of aging that most women will tend to lose the soft skin and perhaps increase body fat as they mature. As husbands we need to cherish our wives through these transitions, whatever changes to their appearance and body shape occur—and vice-versa!!

When we start dating, our natural thought process is to impress and to make ourselves worthy of each other. Saturday night was preening night. I would take ages to choose what to wear. Would these shoes go with that skirt? Does this blouse look baggy and too see through? Disco lights were notorious for lighting up your underwear!

On the night that I met Kevin, I was happily dancing with my best friend and college mate. Suddenly I felt a gentle touch on my arm and there stood, in front of me, this guy who, as I said before appeared shorter than myself. I hadn't, of course, taken into consideration that I had chosen to put on my black stiletto heels that night. Power dressing Kevin calls it - well it worked! He thought he'd taken on a real challenge! Kevin was, in my opinion, very handsomely dressed in a jacket that complimented his dark purple shirt. I also noted how dreamy his eyes were, how dark, soft and shiny his hair fell, just over his collar. I could go on but the point I'm coming to is that we had both made the effort to impress and attract. And this continued throughout our courtship, or should I say our dating days. We both wanted to show our love to and for each other. It wasn't that we just cared about how we looked but we cared about each other's interests too. I wanted to please Kevin and share in what he enjoyed and he was the same towards me. We were connecting and beginning to cherish and 'fall' in love with each other.

Our interest in dancing continues, to a lesser extent, today. Dancing is actually a great way to illustrate a loving leadership, how a husband is supposed to truly love his wife and the way a wife is to respond, respectfully, to that headship in their marriage.

When you think of Ballroom dancing, you see two people in perfect 'holding' position. The man gently leads the woman around the dance floor. She willingly enjoys his firm embrace and, in turn, he takes pleasure in her beauty and total reliance on him. A man's primary need is to be respected (Ephesians 5:33 and Colossians 3:18/19) and for a woman it is security. The dance shows perfectly this beautiful relationship.

As a Christian, I believe the ultimate dance teacher, who instructs us how to do the steps properly, is God Himself. Isn't it wonderful that He created this marriage pattern in which the Bible describes as a 'template' for us, to reflect Christ's relationship with His church—that's us who believe? I suggest you look it up for yourselves in Paul's letters to the Ephesians as well as the Colossians. (See above) In essence, to truly love someone, it has to be a gift, a voluntary act of giving yourself for the sake of the other; for the husband, it's sacrificial leadership;

for the wife, it is recognising his manly strength in a loving, protective way by feeling his firm arm around her waist, so that when she follows his steps around the dance floor they will not feel lost or alone and fall down in a heap together! For them both, it is to show love in a tender, affectionate and submissive way, emphasising their enjoyment of each other with a deep need and respect between them.

The word submission in Greek actually means to 'place oneself under'. By submitting to one another in mutual respect, we are fulfilling the vow to love, honour and cherish. A wife is responsible to her husband, her husband is responsible to Christ, Christ is responsible to God. (1 Corinthians 11:3) Husband and wife are not independent from one another but interdependent towards one another. This was God's plan. This is how we honour. 'To honour,' means to really value something or someone. It means to attach great worth towards that person like you would value gold. There is a weighty cost to your relationship as true love is worth working at. In contrast, to dishonour is to treat that person with little or no weight or value, as if the relationship was as thin as a mist—a mere vapour; that is contemptuous. When we speak in critical tones, putting our husband or wife down, surely that is treating them with dishonour. What happened to those loving, affirming words? One might as well dance back to back, on opposite sides of the room! Where is the intimacy in the marriage when there is no loving submission and no honour?

When Kevin and I performed the Rumba in Weston-super-Mare's Winter Gardens, three years ago, we decided to start at each end of the dance floor and meet in the middle. If you have ever been there or indeed any large, proper ballroom, you will appreciate how vast the space between us was. To begin with, when the music began, we moved slowly towards each other until at last we could hold and help each other to continue the routine. I think we both felt very conspicuous and vulnerable when left alone at the beginning, but when we came together it highlighted the intimacy that should be found in the Rumba dance, known affectionately as the 'Dance of Love.' There is a dance that does quite the opposite to the loving, intimate dance of mutual respect, submission and honouring. It is the dance of intimidation. Fear is what happens when people, particularly couples, get into conflict due to miscommunication. It leads to hurt as a result of each person 'pressing' each other's sensitive 'button'. They are reacting to a deep, inner fear or hurt by being hurtful back, in the hope that their partner will give them what they want to counteract their feelings. This usually stems from their upbringing. Having just retaliated by pushing their partner's sensitive button, they find themselves going around and around with neither backing down but trying to win.[xi] More like a Paso Doble than a Waltz, the dance gets into a circular motion of scoring points—get the picture?

How does it all stop? Well, as we all know it's usually in tears, with slamming of doors, the silent treatment or with a stream of further dishonouring abuse.

Another great writer and speaker on marriage issues, who we have the pleasure of knowing and meeting on many occasions, and have learnt a lot from over the years, is Harry Benson. He was founder of the Bristol Community Family Trust and now the Director of Research for the Marriage Foundation. He produced a useful way of trying to prevent the 'fear dance' in the first place by creating the anagram S.T.O.P The first two letters of the anagram are the beginnings of the dance— S for scoring points (a kind of one-upmanship) and then T for thinking the worst about our spouse. Being negative about their intentions and character. The last two letters continue the dance or end it badly. They are O for opting out or just leaving the argument to an inconclusive hiatus, which just makes the remaining spouse feel rejected and confused. The last is P for putting down. I will admit that I am guilty of this 'bad habit' as

Harry refers to them.[xii] I have a tendency towards being sarcastic with the last word—not happy to let Kevin 'win'—especially if my character has been maligned by Kevin's bad habit of thinking the worst of me. We are both agreed that we are good at scoring points like two lawyers in a court room believing they both are right, giving their final summing up speeches with their own verdict.

We know deep down that no one 'wins' or 'loses' because we are on the same team. We are meant to love, support and encourage each other.

Habits are all too easy to pick up so it is better to learn good ones—which should destroy the bad ones or at least make them less frequent. What did we all do when we first met our husband and wife? We made the effort to attract them. We honoured them with our best behaviour, our kind words. We showed an interest in getting to know them. It took time and it cost us because we valued them and still do because we love them. Love is a verb. It is an active word. In 1 Corinthians chapter 13, known as the love chapter and often read at weddings, it says, "Love is patient and kind…it is faithful, hopeful and endures through every circumstance." (NLT)

Kevin and I spent ten weeks learning and practicing our dance routine before performing it in the Winter Gardens in Weston-super-Mare, our hometown in North Somerset. Over the weeks we thought we would never 'get it.' We kept forgetting the routine or worst still, one of us would forget when the other remembered and vice-versa. So, we both had a chance to shoot dishonouring words and put downs at each other but I have to say it was mainly done in a playful way because we realised, like a marriage, you're in it together. We both had to make it work. We laughed so much sometimes that it was almost too difficult to stand still. It was encouraging to see and hear the stories of other competitors—couples, from our church, who were also struggling like us but enjoying the challenge to get it right.

We believe Jesus is the Lord of the Dance. He leads us and guides us if we let Him and He reminds us of how we should show true love that is unconditional, submissive and honouring—the way it was in the beginning.

Let's Pray

1. For my wife/husband every day. Ask them what they would like to be prayed for. Ask God to help, protect and guide them throughout the day and night.

2. Ask God to show us how to submit to one another - loving each other with honour and respect. Putting our husband /wife first in thought and deed. Let us ask the Lord of the Dance.
3. For our children—together. Let us pray as a couple, recognising the importance of keeping our vows for their sakes as well as our own and not placing our children above our husband/wife in an obsessive manner.
4. For our sexual union as a married couple—help us Lord to really cherish and honour the marriage bed with the giving of our bodies, without shame or lust but with pure love and affection

Chapter 7

Till death Do Us Part

'Love never gives up, never loses faith, is always hopeful, and endures through every circumstance' (1 Corinthians 13: 7) NLT

I saw a phrase that described marriage as a 'long lasting alliance between two people that is expected to last a lifetime.'
This vow appears to encompass all the vows put together; It is a very strong vow expressing our decision to be together and to holdfast through all the pain and joy in the good times and in the bad, to bring our best and forgive our worst, to tentatively pick ourselves up in the lean years and count our blessings in relatively wealthy times. When we are going through tough days of ill health, we are able to look back and give thanks for the healthy years. When we are loving and cherishing with submissive respect towards each other, only then can we see ourselves being able to fix our eyes on the prize that we can

endure to the end when death parts us physically. Yes, it is saying we are committed until the end when we will part.

It is the 'do us part' bit that I want to address first because many people believe that we remain married when we have both died. In our village we have a small cemetery that is linked to our beautiful little Anglican church, quite near to where we live. I often choose to walk through this cemetery, along a narrow path that winds its way up from the village high street, up some steps, to the 'top' road where our house is. There is a serenity that I find looking at the names and ages of those that have lived before. I imagine what they were like as people and what sort of lives they led. However, one of the things I have noted is the number of years between the death of one spouse who dies first—usually the husband (sorry guys) and the death of the remaining spouse. Many wives have been widowed longer than they were married and many seem not to have remarried. The epitaph often says, 'Together again' or 'United in death' or something similar. It's very touching but is it true?

The phrase 'to part,' a verb, which actually means to separate, split and move apart is, of course, the opposite to being joined together. God 'joins' us one with another so, 'the two are united into one' (Genesis 2:24, Matthew 19:5, Ephesians 5:31 NLT) In this way, what God has 'joined' only He can part or separate.

When couples divorce, they may part ways but they haven't really parted completely. What do I mean by this? Well, a good and thought-provoking illustration is the one that is done on 'The Marriage course', which shows the effects of divorce and its implications. Take two pieces of paper (a blue and a pink one?) and join them equally with glue until they have stuck fast. When trying to pull the two pieces apart, you are left with bits of blue and pink paper on both sheets. In other words, when man is involved in the separation of two married people, he or she leaves a lot of hurt and mess. This is further complicated if the couple have children for whom that they will continue to share responsibility when the couple separate. If they remarry, there is a great deal of adjustment for potential step-parenting. They can never really finally leave or 'part' each other except when God actually parts them through death. Death is what separates.

In spiritual terms, we are all separated from God in our 'polluted unbelief and…disobedience' (Ephesians 2:2 THE MESSAGE). Now, for some of you this is becoming too theological! Please stay with me as we try to connect our understanding with this vow. When we 'give our lives', that is saying "yes" to Jesus Christ and recognising Him as our Lord and Saviour of our lives, we are no longer 'dead' in our own thoughts and ways of doing things, bound by the 'law' of this natural world. We are instead made 'alive' and set 'free' because He died for us and then arose again to defeat death and separation from God. We are a 'new creation' spiritually speaking.

In the book of Romans, Paul uses marriage to explain this mystery of our salvation, by pointing out that while a woman is married to her husband she is bound or legally tied to him, by law, but only when he dies is she 'free' to marry again. (Romans 7:2-3). In this age of 'making it fair' for both men and women, this scripture applies to the husband as well!

When you think about it, our sins are highlighted in marriage like God's 'law' highlights our disobedience. We are tested by each other and not always the best of us is revealed! Thank God for his grace!

So, what happens then, as a married couple, when we both die? What does Jesus himself say about it? Why do we say 'til death do us part'? In the Gospels of Luke, Matthew and Mark, Jesus confronts the Sadducees, a group of conservative religious leaders, who believed that death was the end of existence—there was no resurrection or eternal life. Jesus quickly corrects their ignorance of the scriptures and that they 'don't know the power of God' (Mark 12:24, Matt 22:29 NLT) He continues to explain that those 'worthy of being raised…won't be married.' And 'For when the dead rise, they won't be married. They will be like the Angels in Heaven.' (Luke 20:35-36 & Matt 22:30 NLT)

In B.W Johnson's Bible commentary on Matthew's Gospel, referring to the same comment made by Jesus to the Sadducees, he infers that when we, as followers of Christ, are taken up to be with Him, we will be like the angels, only having spiritual interaction without bodily intimacy. He believes that physical relationships, like that of marriage, will not belong to our spiritual makeup. The Message Bible translates this 'As with the angels, all our ecstasies and intimacies then will be with God.' (Luke 20:28 THE MESSAGE)

Marriage was God's design for companionship as well as co-working and reproduction of the human race. (Genesis 2:18 & 21-24). But Jesus had to explain to the religious leaders of his day and thereby to us, that there are no sexual relationships or indeed exclusivity among us in Heaven—we will be like the angels experiencing the power and glory of our resurrected, spiritual bodies, that have been renewed and transformed into Christ-likeness. There is a somewhat lengthy explanation in 1 Corinthians chapter 15 (verses 35-45) where St Paul provides some insight into what it will be like for us in heaven. In other scripture, for example in Luke (chapter 16 verse 23) where Jesus is illustrating a point through one of His parables or stories, there is a hint that we will recognise our earthly husbands and wives as well as others but the same physical and natural rules do not apply in heaven. Here on earth, we are confined by time, place and man-made ideas and we must make sure that we do not think of heaven as an extension of earth because it will be far beyond our greatest expectations!

While we are still looking at marriage in the context of the afterlife and the 'do us part' bit of the vow, I feel it is worthy of mention to include a quick note of Paul's description of the marriage union in Ephesians (Ch 5:25-32). He says that the husband and wife relationship should closely mirror or illustrate Christ's relationship with us—His church. In Heaven however, when we have died and parted from our spouse, there will be no need for our marriages to be an illustration, a copy or reflection. Jesus will be our bridegroom, our husband. We will be His 'bride' and the wedding feast will take place in Heaven, (Revelation 19:7-9).

I have spent some time looking at this aspect of the vow to not only help us understand why it is said but also to fully take on board the spiritual significance of the joining by God, when we marry and that it is until death. It is first declared by God in the garden (Genesis 2:24) and Jesus applies it in two of the Gospels (Matt 19:4-6 & Mark 10:7-9) before referencing again in Ephesians (Ch 5:31-32). In my opinion, it seems reasonable to believe that it is an important point to make.

Now let us move on to consider the 'until death' bit.

When a young couple are standing face to face, as Kevin and I did over thirty years ago, stating that vow, 'until death do us part', it feels incomprehensible at that moment in time. It's a lifetime away isn't it?... or so it seems. We often suggest to engaged couples, when they come to us for their marriage preparation, that they just stop and think for a while and paint or draw a picture, quite literary sometimes, or imagine a photo (not their wedding photo) of themselves in twenty, thirty or even in fifty years. There is often a chuckle and a look of surprise, possibly horror mixed with a little sense of bewilderment at the thought of so many years away, especially the fifty. But very soon the dreams and aspirations of their lives together create that excitement and determination that they are going to make this marriage last. That is what this vow also brings to mind. It highlights the readiness of the couple and their prompt compliance and willingness to accept this new status- they are together for life—until death.

What a vow! We must be careful what we are saying. We can easily forget that there is power in our words and if you have faith in God—He puts great emphasis on oath taking, vow breaking—'But once you have voluntarily made a vow, be careful to do as you have said (for it was your own choice) for you have made a vow to the Lord your God' (Deuteronomy 23:23 NLT)

I read an article the other day by Pastor Sam Crabtree of Minneapolis, Minnesota.[xiii] It was called 'Until death do us part for real.' He wrote very bluntly when he implied that when death is the only option for a marriage to end, then don't promise 'until death' when you make your wedding vows. He went on to remind us all about truth telling and to always promise what we mean because God cannot lie (Titus 1:2) and He delights in those who tell the truth and keep their oaths. (Ecclesiastes 5:4 -5)

It's not as easy in practice! I don't need to tell you that life is hard. It is confusing and sometimes, in our eyes, completely unfair. For some (and we know a few people) life has not gone the way they planned it. Keeping the vow, 'until death' was seemingly impossible. King Solomon observes in his writings in Ecclesiastes, 'Even though the actions of Godly and wise people are in God's hands, no one knows whether or not God will show them favour in this life. The same destiny ultimately awaits everyone…' (Ch 9:1 & 2)

The commands of God are given because that is what God intended for our lives. These are what Paul called them in 1 Corinthians 7:10 and in the Gospels (Matt 5:32, Luke 16:18 & Mark 10:11,12) But since we fell from a right relationship with our creator, creation too has fallen. Everybody and everything are far from perfect. But there is good news! Jesus is perfect and took our fallen nature on Himself when He died and rose again. If we seek His forgiveness for breaking this vow (or you have been a victim and been caused to break it), then He is a loving God of infinite forgiveness and only desires what is best for you. King Solomon also reminds us that, 'even though a person sins a hundred times and still lives a long time, I know that those who fear God will be better off.' (Ch 8:12 NLT)

We love attending weddings and in our ministry with engaged couples, we have had the privilege of being invited to a fair few. It's heart-warming to observe them as they meet together at the altar and say their vows. (It is with this in mind that partly prompted us to write this book!) This is when all the wedding party come together. They are serious for a few minutes as they listen to the couple and are aware of their role as witnesses to the solemn oaths being sworn. At that time, those of us who took those vows, recently or many years since, have an opportunity to reminisce, to give thanks or even to quietly reaffirm our vows to each other. It is good to recollect, re-adjust and sometimes reconcile in order to continue moving on together.

Recognising the importance of sticking together through 'thick and thin' not only affirms our resolve and gives strength to our relationship, but it also encourages those around us. It brings hope and aspiration, not only to the younger generation, but to all ages. To coin an appropriate phrase for this chapter, "at the end of the day." we are not here for ourselves but to be a blessing to others.

There was a German pastor called Dietrich Bonhoeffer who was imprisoned during the war for his opposition to Hitler and the Third Reich. It was during this time that he wrote a letter for his niece, who was getting married. He would have taken the service if he'd been free, so he wrote it like a sermon and it was smuggled out and read out at her wedding. This part of the letter illustrates the fact that our marriage is more than we realise and therefore worth working out until death parts us. He wrote, 'You have just said to one another "I will" and with those words you have declared your voluntary assent and turned a critical point in your lives…', he continued. Marriage is more than your love for each other. It has a higher dignity and power for it is God's Holy ordinance through which He wills to perpetuate the human race until the end of time. In your love you see only your two selves in the world but in your marriage you are a link in the chain of the generations, which God causes to come and to pass away to His Glory and calls into His Kingdom. In your love you see only the heaven of your happiness but in marriage you are placed at a post of responsibility towards the world and mankind. Your love is your own private possession, but marriage is more than something personal—it is a status, an office.'[xiv]

Take a moment to re-read that and absorb its meaning. It is very significant and certainly makes Kevin and I feel very blessed to be married but at the same time, gives us a huge sense of responsibility. Maybe we should take it seriously and do everything to keep our marriages alive and beautiful so others are drawn to the concept of getting married and grasping its importance.

Most people like to travel or at least explore somewhere different, even if it's not too far. Most people like picking up a good book because of the 'what is going to happen next' feeling. Actually, having an interesting story to read whilst travelling is a great combination—there is an air of excitement and adventure about both. Where am I going with this?

Well, getting married and saying the vows is like stepping out and starting a new journey and your lives are at the beginning, on the first pages, of a great novel that is just being written. Like all journeys and books there is a beginning, a middle part but also the end. Wouldn't you find it frustrating if you never got to your expected destination? Or when you got towards the end of the book, you find the last few pages had been ripped out? That sense of loss or emptiness, even anger or frustration, doesn't need to be there if we have decided to do whatever it takes to help our marriage along the way. Taking that different, more bumpy, bendy path instead of the smooth, straight, predictable highway, means the journey might be more edgy but you will grow stronger together and your marriage will be more interesting! Isn't that what you want?

Speaking of bumpy roads, that has just reminded me of a time when travelling with Kevin and his parents on a holiday in Norfolk. A shortcut to Ely took us along a very bouncy and narrow lane. My only memory of it now is all the laughter it created as we bobbed up and down on our car seats and arrived in Ely with tears of joy!

And as for the missing pages of the book—have you ever wondered what could happen? What plans God has in store? Dream dreams together and have fun!

You could be reading this in the 'empty nest'—as we are—and there can still be a thrill and excitement in our marriages during this time. We are to be totally open, like a book, expressing ourselves in every avenue of our lives, physically, emotionally and spiritually.

In 'The Marriage Book,' Nicky and Silla Lee write, 'the marriage relationship is designed by God to be an adventure of love that lasts a life time.' They remind us that, 'marriage is designed by God to be a relationship in which a man and a woman give themselves to each other in radical and total abandonment.'[xv] That has to be with lots of laughter and enjoyment of each other and this can only be fully understood on the firm foundation of the marriage covenant—the vow of commitment—until death do us part. We forget that these vows, these promises are not said and signed on 'just a piece of paper'. A covenant is more meaningful than a contract. It is based on our will and choosing. Choosing to love God's way-which is sure, reliable and permanent. It's that firm, secure foundation that Jesus spoke of in the Gospel of Luke 6:48. Those who hear His words and put them into practice 'are like a smart carpenter who dug deep and laid the foundations of his house on bedrock. When the river burst its banks and crashed against the house, nothing could shake it; it was built to last.'(THE MESSAGE)

> *'Place me like a seal over your heart, or like a seal on your arm. For love is as strong as death and its jealousy is enduring as the grave. Love flashes like fire, the brightest kind of flame. Many waters cannot quench love, neither can rivers drown it.' (Song of Songs 8:6, 7 NLT)*

I made mention of the empty nest stage earlier, also referred to as a season of marriage. Yes, we could say that marriages go through four seasons and we grow, hopefully, towards each other but we don't all experience each season. The first season, spring, is the honeymoon phase. It is a time to build on our friendship and get to know and accept each other's differences. Some couples may have already by-passed this by bringing children into the marriage that they may have had from a previous relationship or as a cohabitating couple—so they go straight into summer. The summer is the most hectic of all the seasons, bringing added pressure to the relationship. It is the most active and busiest because of young children and the couple are possibly juggling their careers with running a home. Autumn doesn't get much better. It's changeable and stormy with teenagers and young adults making their voices heard but still expecting Mum and Dad to help them. Similar to summer, autumn can have a couple spend too much time on the children and their increasing emotional needs. The couple are then neglecting their own need for intimacy and enjoyment of the marriage relationship. It is a real test to see how firm the foundation is and how much love and understanding is shown between the couple.

When winter comes along—the empty nest stage—it is hoped that there would have been enough time and care invested into the relationship to help it last the lifetime that the couple vowed to keep. The winter season is less active, giving more opportunities for couples to 'do' things together and increase their knowledge and friendship for each other. For surely the ultimate purpose for our marriage is that we become so 'one flesh,' both growing in the knowledge of God as well as one another.

There is a lovely description of how we become one, as we move forwards together in our marriage, over a lifetime. In the words of John Bayley about his marriage to the author Iris Murdoch, he said, "Looking back, I separate us with difficulty. We seem always to have been together...But where Iris is concerned, my own memory, like a snug-fitting garment, seems to have zipped itself up to the present second...I know she must once have been different, but I have no true memory of a different person."[xvi] I warm to the understanding of that part where he recalls being 'zipped' together like a 'snug-fitting garment.' Apart from someone whom you truly love like your husband or wife, one can't get much closer to another person quite like that can you? It reminds me of St Paul's words in his letter to the Colossians.

> *'Clothe yourselves with tender-hearted mercy, kindness, humility, gentleness and patience...the most important piece of clothing you must wear is love.' (Ch 3:12,14 NLT)*

All these attributes will be fulfilled and perfected in ourselves but will take time—a lifetime!

Author Timothy Keller, in his book, 'The Meaning of Marriage' writes 'What, then, is marriage for? It is for helping each other to become our future glory-selves, the new creations that God will eventually make us. The common horizon husband and wife look towards is the throne, and the Holy, spotless, and blameless nature we will have. I can think of no more powerful common horizon than that, and that is why putting a Christian friendship at the heart of marriage can lift it to a level that no other vision for marriage approaches.'[xvii]

Investing time and interest in one another is so vitally important before we reach that winter season. I was just listening to actress Prunella Scales on a television programme the other day. She, too, has sadly become another victim of Alzheimer's disease but during her fifty years of marriage to husband and fellow actor Timothy West, they spent many wonderful years exploring the canals together and to her it is even more important that they look forward to the years ahead of them—together.

'Therefore, we do not lose heart. Though outwardly we are wasting away, yet inwardly we are being renewed day by day. For our light and momentary troubles are achieving for us an eternal glory that far outweighs them all. Therefore, we fix our eyes not on what is seen, but what is unseen.' (2 Corinthians 4:16-18 NLT)

It is those 'momentary troubles,' those tests of our love and friendship that help to mould us. The founder and chairman of 'Care for the Family' Rob Parsons has written many books on marriage and family life in which he takes the theme of 'seasons' in our marriages, speaking of a 'January love.' January, in the U.K, is a cold, grey and a somewhat drab month after the excitement of Christmas in December. Some couples fear that dull, depressing and potentially inactive time in their marriage when children are no longer around and they appear to have nothing to talk about. Rob says, 'You have to learn to love not just on summer days when the sun is shining and the birds are singing, but in January too.'[xviii]

If we are helping and encouraging one another to become 'all' that God plans for us to be; if we have learned to accept the fact that our husband or wife will change through the years as we spend time enjoying their company, sharing and appreciating their interests, then the winter can be a beautiful, crisp and sparkling time. January can be the start of something exciting—every year!

The vow, 'until death do us part' must not be confused with the fairy tale ending 'live happily ever after.' The 'happily' bit sounds fluffy having recognised that there are tough times and trials which can actually bring us closer together or drive us apart if there is no strong, firm foundation of committed love on which to stand our relationship. Happy equals happenings that 'happen' now and again; an up and down existence where there is no deep inner joy and security.

In a relationship like marriage, a firm foundation of committed love is created by making wise decisions to love at all costs. In the story of 'Captain Corelli's Mandolin,'[xix] the writer, Louis de Bernières, describes this nature of love through the character of Doctor Iannis, speaking to his daughter Pelagia about his own experiences. The father gently guides her thoughts away from giving up so easily when trouble comes. His words suggest how intricately woven, like tangled roots, our lives can become in a marriage, that it would be unthinkable to even consider separating.

I heard some simple but thought-provoking words said in a film the other night. It went something like, "Nobody is perfect— we don't get a perfect partner. All relationships struggle, it's just deciding who you are going to struggle with." That last statement of fact… 'Who are you going to struggle with?' Who are we going to be committed to until death? Let us not struggle against one another. Let us instead get so used to each other's quirky idiosyncrasies and irritating habits that they even make us smile. Last night I noticed that Kevin had managed to walk past the ironing board, which I had still left out after putting the ironed 'pile' away and placed the iron itself in the kitchen to cool down. Kevin had acknowledged this but still walked past the said ironing board to get to the lounge sofa before me, as I was making tea. "Didn't you see it? Couldn't you have put it away for me?" I asked rather disappointingly.

He came up with two or three 'excuses' but then realised I had caught him out when I jokingly asked which one he was going to choose! I was in stitches of laughter, which made him laugh and the potential conflict was abated. I have got so used to Kevin's ability to overlook things and know he doesn't do it deliberately to annoy me. He just has a 'man brain' with less peripheral vision than us ladies! (I think we all know what I mean!) There is also the story of the serial drawer opener, who drove her husband mad until one day he came to a momentous decision that he would just close the drawer each time and say nothing— (think I've covered all gender stereotypes?)

We must pick out carefully what is worth making a fuss about. Kevin doesn't shout to me anymore but makes faces through the dining room window as I'm hanging out the washing in the garden, having left the back door open for the millionth and one time, letting a cold blast blow through the house. And I have given up asking Kevin to wipe the end of his electric toothbrush properly, so it doesn't make a sloppy puddle on the windowsill. I simply do it myself as part of my cleaning routine. My OCD tendency is satisfied!

There are two other great irritations of mine that have nothing to do with my dear and very understanding husband (really!); one of them occurs in the bathroom, but the other is in the garden. You may even have them as well…lime scale and bindweed! I feel there must be an analogy here.

We started this book in a garden so it is fitting to finish there too. Marriage began in a garden and ends in one as well.

My marriage could be like lime scale and bindweed. I could think of all the negatives aspects of my life whenever I get frustrated with my husband and my 'lot.' Bindweed that tangles itself around all the pretty plants and shrubs and just about manages to wind itself through every nook and cranny of the raised borders, could be a metaphor of my feelings of being strangled by Kevin's need for my presence when I need space and could feel suffocated. I could see it as a real nuisance every time I have to refer to him with our finances or any plans I want to make. Some wives feel 'tied' to the housework. Similarly, like lime scale, our conversations might get sticky due to bad listening habits from a hard build up of bad attitudes. There may be a blockage where unforgiveness has clogged up the channels of communication and been left to get trapped in the plugholes of our parallel lives. It continues to harden our hearts towards each other until we no longer see ourselves as we once did because of the "calcium carbonate" of mistrust, anger and bitterness, building layer by layer and eventually like a kitchen appliance, it breaks down.

Or—I could see the positives.

When we got married, we were 'bound' together symbolically by the vicar when he placed a part of his stole over our hands and said "What God has joined together, let no one separate." We had already agreed in our vows that it would mean until death. We hold together, we think alike and we have a close association in mind, body and spirit. The dictionary describes the word 'binding' as a duty. Haven't we already looked at that with Bonhoeffer's sermon to his niece? Binding also means 'to be subject to legal obligations.' That is our promised covenant that God has witnessed 'You were united to your wife by the Lord...the two of you became one person in His sight.' (Malachi 2:15)

Let us think back to that earlier suggestion of our marriage becoming stronger as we grow closer together. We become so entwined that our roots become one. Bindweed—a convolvulus, twining plant coils and rolls together, it is deeply rooted. Interestingly, the bindweed plant is sometimes thought of as being in the same family as the honeysuckle, creeping upwards and coiling around a stem. Apparently, this is not so as it coils in the opposite direction. The honeysuckle, however does smell sweet and reminds me of a verse in 2 Corinthians 2:14 & 15. Our lives and our marriages are to give off the sweet fragrance of

Jesus from them. Here is another observation about the flower of the bindweed. Look at the beautiful, white, trumpet-like flowers; a symbol of purity and love. We have the responsibility to be the bedrock of society if we want a better world to live in. Let us shout it from the rooftops as a trumpet sound!

And lime scale? Well, again, the dictionary describes it as having cleansing, protecting and strengthening properties. (I am aware that those of us who have hard water due to lime scale, experience better health and stronger teeth!) Research has shown that couples in happy and strong marriages experience better health and potentially live longer![xx]

Our love for each other, like St Paul describes in 1 Corinthians 13:7, is all about faithful, committed, 'until death do us part love.' He is saying, that there is nothing love cannot face, there is no limit to its faith, its hope, its endurance. Real love goes on to the end of time.

Let's Pray

1. For a determined spirit of willingness to do all that is necessary to keep this vow of commitment because this is what marriage is all about—until we die.

2. For the season of marriage that we are in. Pray for God's help to endure, to love against the odds and to enjoy each other through it all.
3. For a positive outlook for each other. Moving forward towards the end, clothing ourselves in humility until we are zipped together in harmony, until death parts us.
4. For an understanding of what it means to be 'saved' and 'made alive'- to be 'set free.' If you are not a Christian then speak to a friend who is, or a local minister, and ask.
5. For a true understanding of a 'Marriage made in Heaven'.

Epilogue

"Where there is no revelation people cast off restraint;" (Proverbs 29a:18 NIV)

Do you have a personal vision for your marriage? A shared dream, a purpose or destiny? Does it include family, a home, a happy life, success, prosperity and fulfilment? Whatever your vision is, can we encourage you to write it down in words or sketched pictures and share it with your spouse or fiancé(e)? We realise that for many this may be challenging. It may be that you just take life as it comes or you feel that it seems unrealistic or even too prescriptive to map things out. We have found that having a vision helps with choices and direction. Being honest, we probably didn't have much of a vision when we started, besides indulging in each other's company and settling down. But more recently we have found it more helpful to work out what we both want and need in our time remaining here on earth. We would recommend that this vision is regularly re-visited at least every 5 years, if not every year, as our circumstances may vary beyond our control. Our preferences will change with time so articulating these frequently will help us check that we are headed in the same direction. We believe that the best way to develop a vision for your marriage, is by praying about it together and asking God to speak to us individually. We then wait for agreement between us all. It is not so much about asking God to bless the vision we have determined for ourselves, but more about listening and aligning our vision with God and writing it down. Are we willing to be directed in our prayers so that we can be more useful to Him? There may be compromises, disappointments or even disagreements about the journey, but we believe having a plan, however vague, is better than having regrets.

Will you join us with our vision to keep traditional marriage on the map of our society? Will you value it, cherish it and support and encourage others by getting word out in the world that marriage does matter? Will you help us with an army of others that feel the same, to put out the message that marriage is aspirational, is good, something to be worked at, and encouraged rather than an out-dated model for the 'lucky few'?

For more information contact either Kevin or Mandy at info@themarriagepartnership.org.uk

If you enjoyed this book and purchased it online please help us by writing a review on the same website that you purchased it from. This will help it get a higher ranking amongst books of a similar theme. Thank you!

Appendix A.1

The Marriage Service

Introduction

The Welcome

The minister welcomes the people using these or other appropriate words

The grace of our Lord Jesus Christ,

the love of God,

and the fellowship of the Holy Spirit

be with you

All ***and also with you.***

This sentence may be used

God is love, and those who live in love live in God

and God lives in them.

I John 4.16

This prayer may be said

All ***God of wonder and of joy:***

grace comes from you,

and you alone are the source of life and love.

Without you, we cannot please you;

without your love, our deeds are worth nothing.

Send your Holy Spirit,
and pour into our hearts
that most excellent gift of love,
that we may worship you now
with thankful hearts
and serve you always with willing minds;
through Jesus Christ our Lord.
Amen.

A hymn may be sung.

Preface

These words or an alternative preface may be used

In the presence of God, Father, Son and Holy Spirit,
we have come together
to witness the marriage of *N* and *N*,
to pray for God's blessing on them,
to share their joy
and to celebrate their love.

Marriage is a gift of God in creation
through which husband and wife may know the grace of God.
It is given
that as man and woman grow together in love and trust,

they shall be united with one another in heart, body and mind,
as Christ is united with his bride, the Church.

The gift of marriage brings husband and wife together
in the delight and tenderness of sexual union
and joyful commitment to the end of their lives.
It is given as the foundation of family life
in which children are [born and] nurtured
and in which each member of the family,
in good times and in bad,
may find strength, companionship and comfort,
and grow to maturity in love.

Marriage is a way of life made holy by God,
and blessed by the presence of our Lord Jesus Christ
with those celebrating a wedding at Cana in Galilee.
Marriage is a sign of unity and loyalty
which all should uphold and honour.
It enriches society and strengthens community.
No one should enter into it lightly or selfishly
but reverently and responsibly in the sight of almighty God.

N and *N* are now to enter this way of life.
They will each give their consent to the other

and make solemn vows,
and in token of this they will [each] give and receive a ring.
We pray with them that the Holy Spirit will guide and strengthen them, that they may fulfil God's purposes for the whole of their earthly life together.

The Declarations

The minister says to the congregation

First, I am required to ask anyone present who knows a reason why these persons may not lawfully marry, to declare it now.

The minister says to the couple

The vows you are about to take are to be made in the presence of God, who is judge of all and knows all the secrets of our hearts;
therefore if either of you knows a reason why you may not lawfully marry, you must declare it now.

The minister says to the bridegroom

N, will you take *N* to be your wife?
Will you love her, comfort her, honour and protect her,
and, forsaking all others,
be faithful to her as long as you both shall live?

He answers

I will.

The minister says to the bride

N, will you take *N* to be your husband?

Will you love him, comfort him, honour and protect him,

and, forsaking all others,

be faithful to him as long as you both shall live?

She answers

I will.

The minister says to the congregation

Will you, the families and friends of *N* and *N*,

support and uphold them in their marriage

now and in the years to come?

All ***We will.***

The Collect

The minister invites the people to pray, silence is kept and the minister says the Collect

God our Father,

from the beginning

you have blessed creation with abundant life.

Pour out your blessings upon *N* and *N*,

that they may be joined in mutual love and companionship,

in holiness and commitment to each other.

We ask this through our Lord Jesus Christ your Son,

who is alive and reigns with you,
in the unity of the Holy Spirit,
one God, now and for ever.
All *Amen.*

Readings

At least one reading from the Bible is used.

Sermon

The Marriage

A hymn may be sung.
The couple stand before the minister.

The Vows

The minister introduces the vows in these or similar words
N and *N*, I now invite you to join hands and make your vows,
in the presence of God and his people.

The bride and bridegroom face each other.
The bridegroom takes the bride's right hand in his.
These words are used or Form 1 or 2

I, *N*, take you, *N*,
to be my wife,
to have and to hold
from this day forward;

for better, for worse,

for richer, for poorer,

in sickness and in health,

to love and to cherish,

till death us do part;

according to God's holy law.

In the presence of God I make this vow.

They loose hands.

The bride takes the bridegroom's right hand in hers, and says

I, *N*, take you, *N*,

to be my husband,

to have and to hold

from this day forward;

for better, for worse,

for richer, for poorer,

in sickness and in health,

to love and to cherish,

till death us do part;

according to God's holy law.

In the presence of God I make this vow.

They loose hands.

The Giving of Rings

The minister receives the ring(s), and says this or an alternative prayer

Heavenly Father, by your blessing

let these rings be to *N* and *N*

a symbol of unending love and faithfulness,

to remind them of the vow and covenant

which they have made this day

through Jesus Christ our Lord.

All *Amen.*

The bridegroom places the ring on the fourth finger of the bride's left hand and, holding it there, says

N, I give you this ring

as a sign of our marriage.

With my body I honour you,

all that I am I give to you,

and all that I have I share with you,

within the love of God,

Father, Son and Holy Spirit.

If rings are exchanged, they loose hands and the bride places a ring on the fourth finger of the bridegroom's left hand and, holding it there, says

N, I give you this ring

as a sign of our marriage.

With my body I honour you,

all that I am I give to you,

and all that I have I share with you,

within the love of God,

Father, Son and Holy Spirit.

If only one ring is used, before they loose hands the bride says

N, I receive this ring

as a sign of our marriage.

With my body I honour you,

all that I am I give to you,

and all that I have I share with you,

within the love of God,

Father, Son and Holy Spirit.

The Proclamation

The minister addresses the people

In the presence of God, and before this congregation,

N and N have given their consent

and made their marriage vows to each other.

They have declared their marriage by the joining of hands

and by the giving and receiving of rings.

I therefore proclaim that they are husband and wife.

The minister joins their right hands together and says

Those whom God has joined together let no one put asunder.

The Blessing of the Marriage

The husband and wife kneel. The minister may use the following or alternative blessing

Blessed are you, O Lord our God,
for you have created joy and gladness,
pleasure and delight, love, peace and fellowship.
Pour out the abundance of your blessing
upon *N* and *N* in their new life together.
Let their love for each other be a seal upon their hearts
and a crown upon their heads.
Bless them in their work and in their companionship;
awake and asleep,
in joy and in sorrow,
in life and in death.
Finally, in your mercy, bring them to that banquet
where your saints feast for ever in your heavenly home.
We ask this through Jesus Christ your Son, our Lord,
who lives and reigns with you and the Holy Spirit,
one God, now and for ever.
All **Amen.**

The minister says to the couple

God the Father,
God the Son,

God the Holy Spirit,

bless, preserve and keep you;

the Lord mercifully grant you the riches of his grace,

that you may please him both in body and soul,

and, living together in faith and love,

may receive the blessings of eternal life.

All *Amen.*

Registration of the Marriage

A hymn or psalm may be used

Prayers

These or other suitable prayers are used. The prayers usually include these concerns and may follow this sequence:

Thanksgiving

Spiritual growth

Faithfulness, joy, love, forgiveness and healing

Children, other family members and friends

Faithful God,

holy and eternal,

source of life and spring of love,

we thank and praise you for bringing N and N to this day,

and we pray for them.

Lord of life and love:

All *hear our prayer.*

May their marriage be life-giving and life-long,
enriched by your presence and strengthened by your grace;
may they bring comfort and confidence to each other
in faithfulness and trust.
Lord of life and love:
All hear our prayer.

May the hospitality of their home
bring refreshment and joy to all around them;
may their love overflow to neighbours in need
and embrace those in distress.
Lord of life and love:
All hear our prayer.

May they discern in your word
order and purpose for their lives;
and may the power of your Holy Spirit
lead them in truth and defend them in adversity.
Lord of life and love:
All hear our prayer.
May they nurture their family with devotion,
see their children grow in body, mind and spirit
and come at last to the end of their lives

with hearts content and in joyful anticipation of heaven.

Lord of life and love:

All *hear our prayer.*

The prayers conclude with the Lord's Prayer.

As our Saviour taught us, so we pray

All *Our Father in heaven,*
hallowed be your name,
your kingdom come,
your will be done,
on earth as in heaven.
Give us today our daily bread.
Forgive us our sins
as we forgive those who sin against us.
Lead us not into temptation
but deliver us from evil.
For the kingdom, the power,
and the glory are yours
now and for ever.
Amen.

(or)

Let us pray with confidence as our Saviour has taught us

All *Our Father, who art in heaven,*
hallowed be thy name;
thy kingdom come;

thy will be done;
on earth as it is in heaven.
Give us this day our daily bread.
And forgive us our trespasses,
as we forgive those who trespass against us.
And lead us not into temptation;
but deliver us from evil.
For thine is the kingdom,
the power and the glory,
for ever and ever.
Amen.

A hymn may be sung.

The Dismissal

The minister says

God the Holy Trinity make you strong in faith and love,
defend you on every side, and guide you in truth and peace;
and the blessing of God almighty,
the Father, the Son, and the Holy Spirit,
be among you and remain with you always.

All *Amen.*

Appendix A.2

Resources

A few of our favourite Marriage Enrichment Courses and marriage resources

In the U.K.

Time for Marriage: https://timeformarriage.org.uk

The Marriage Course & The Marriage Preparation Course: http://themarriagecourses.org

Care for the Family: https://www.careforthefamily.org.uk

In the U.S.A

WinShape Retreat: https://retreat.winshape.org

Married People Resources: http://marriedpeople.org

In Europe

Relateworks (based in Germany): http://www.relateworks.com

Hitched Together (based in Hungary): https://hitchedtogether.com

Bibliography and Notes

[i] The Church of England Marriage Service. (See Appendix A.1)

[ii] Ash, Christopher, (2007), *Married for God*, Nottingham: Inter-varsity Press. © Christopher Ash 2007. "Reproduced with permission of The Licensor through PLSclear."

[iii] Trobisch, Walter, (2005), *I Married You*, Leicester: Inter-Varsity Press.

[iv] Benson, Harry, (2010), *Let's Stick Together*, Oxford: Lion Hudson PLC. ©Care for the Family

[v] Taken from *The Best Yes*, Lysa TerKuerst © Copyright 2014 TerKuerst Foundation. Used by permission of Thomas Nelson. www.thomasnelson.com

[vi] Littauer, Marita, (2014), *Wired That Way*, Grand Rapids: Baker Publishing Group

[vii] Taken from *The Marriage Book: How To Build a Lasting Relationship*, Lee, Nicky and Sila, Copyright © Nicky and Sila 2000. Used by permission of Thomas Nelson. www.thomasnelson.com and Hodder Faith (Hodder & Stoughton)

[viii] http://money.cnn.com/2012/01/04/news/economy/world_richest/index.htm

[ix] https://capuk.org

[x] https://www.psychologytoday.com/gb/articles/200811/in-sickness-and-in-health?collection=60174

[xi] Smalley, Gary, (2004), *The DNA of Relationships*, Illinois, Tyndale House Publishers.

[xii] Benson, Harry, (2010), *Let's Stick Together*, Oxford: Lion Hudson PLC. Copyright ©Care for the Family

[xiii] https://www.desiringgod.org/articles/until-death-do-us-part-for-real

[xiv] taken from *Letters and Papers from Prison* by Dietrich Bonhoeffer, published by SCM Press 1971. Used by permission of Hymns Ancient and Modern Ltd.

[xv] Taken from *The Marriage Book: How To Build a Lasting Relationship*, Lee, Nicky and Sila, Copyright © Nicky and Sila Lee 2000. Used by permission of Thomas Nelson. www.thomasnelson.com and Hodder Faith (Hodder & Stoughton).

[xvi] Bayley, John, Iris, A Memoir of Iris Murdoch (Duckworth 1998) p57, Used by license of Prelude Books Ltd.

[xvii] Keller, Timothy & Kathy, © (2011), *The Meaning of Marriage*: Used by permission of Penguin Random House Publishers US for the USA, its territories and dependencies, the Philippines and Canada and by permission of Hodder and Stoughton UK for the rest of the World.

[xviii] Parsons, Rob, © (2007), *21st Century Marriage: Helpful Hints* booklet used by permission of Care for the Family.

[xix] De Bernières, Louis, (1994), *Captain Corelli's Mandolin,* London: Penguin Random House.

[xx] https://www.telegraph.co.uk/health-fitness/body/the-eight-surprising-health-benefits-of-getting-married

Printed in Great Britain
by Amazon